Getting Your Child Ready for School

Written by Grace Jasmine

Illustrations by Ken Tunell

Teacher Created Materials

Teacher Created Materials, Inc.
P.O. Box 1040
Huntington Beach, CA 92647
©1997 Teacher Created Materials, Inc.
Made in U.S.A.

ISBN-1-57690-128-9

Library of Congress Catalog Card Number: 97-060307

Editor:
Stephanie Buehler, M.P.W., M.A.

Table of Contents

Introduction

Not a Baby Anymore

From your child's first smile to your child's first day of school, you worry about making the right choices. It's natural to be concerned with the well-being of your very special child, and whether you are deciding upon a car seat or his or her education, as a concerned parent, you worry about making the most beneficial choices. You want your son or daughter to be safe, happy, and nurtured, with you or away from you. You want him or her to have opportunities to be successful. You are a parent, and the love you feel for your child can create anxiety about making the happiest, healthiest choices possible.

Baby Bird Leaves the Nest

Whether your child begins his or her educational experience in preschool, kindergarten, or first grade, there are normal developmental expectations for children to achieve before entering school.

Whether your goal for your child is to have him or her fit in with peers or whether your goal is academic achievement, all parents wish to give their children a head start, to make their children's individual educational experiences as positive as possible. But how can you assist your child without causing undue stress or expecting too much too soon?

Developmentally Appropriate Enrichment

The National Association for the Education of Young Children, or NAEYC, has devised what they believe are developmentally appropriate expectations for young children's development from birth through age eight. Popular educational research indicates that there are certain behaviors that are expected for children in certain age ranges. Though these are loose guidelines, they are still helpful.

Throughout Getting Your Child Ready for School, you will find an organized and informative means of assessing your child in four areas:

- Intellectual Readiness
- Physical Readiness
- Emotional Readiness
- Social Readiness

This easy-to-use book takes the guesswork out of school readiness by providing information about how readiness is measured, checklists to help you decide your own child's readiness, and stories and activities for you to use with your child to make his or her beginning school experience as positive as possible.

How The Book Works

Introduction

Early childhood educators agree that young children have different areas in which readiness for school can be assessed. There are certain "norms" that are considered appropriate for proper development in young children from birth through adolescence. While what is "normal" covers a fairly broad range of behaviors, it is valuable to understand what is considered appropriate development for your young child from preschool age through kindergarten and the first grade.

Remember that all children develop differently and, just as parents have concerns over their newborn's development, it is normal to be concerned that your preschooler or kindergartner is developing appropriately. <u>Getting Your Child Ready for School</u> makes it easy for parents to provide assistance or enrichment in achieving optimal development.

Readiness

You may begin using this book by looking over the pages describing the different kinds of readiness. Each section provides condensed and relevant information about the kinds of developmental milestones expected of your child before entering school. These sections will quickly acquaint you with terms and ideas that teachers of young children use in assessment.

Checklists

Use the checklist for each section to determine the current level of your child's development. These checklists are designed to give you a sense of the level of readiness your child has in each of the four areas. You may begin to notice areas of relative strengths and weaknessess. For example, your child may have excellent social skills but lack good coordination. The checklists can help you determine which areas of the book will be the most beneficial.

Stories

Each readiness section has an original children's story to prepare your child for some aspect of school. You and your child will enjoy reading these stories together, while at the same time you will be helping your child get ready for school. Read these stories on a regular basis, copy them from the book, and staple the pages together for books that you can color and use or let your child color the stories right in the book—it's up to you.

How The Book Works *(cont.)*

Activities

In each readiness section, after you and your child read the story, look over the various activities that have been designed to provide enrichment. These interesting activities will motivate you to use everyday materials to create learning experiences that will benefit your child when he or she goes to school. You can either start with the first activity and proceed in order or choose at random. Each activity is designed to stand alone.

Enjoy Life with Your Child

Remember, learning is supposed to be fun, not stressful. Getting Your Child Ready for School has been designed to make your child's beginning school experience more relaxing, rewarding, and enjoyable. Remember that teaching your child is something you will always do. It doesn't stop after your child marches into his or her first day of kindergarten.

Sometimes other people may have a view of your child entirely different from your own. If you do find yourself in this situation, get a second or a third opinion. As parents, it is ultimately your responsibility to ensure that your child is being assessed and treated fairly. See the section on assessment and screening at the end of this book for more help regarding this subject.

It is important to remember your own attitude toward school may be absorbed by your child. Think about the feelings and attitudes you want to project about school to your child and actively express those attitudes you feel will best benefit your child.

And finally, remember that every child is different. Each child's abilities, talents, and learning styles vary. Children are like adults, with different tastes, preferences, opinions, and abilities—they're just a little shorter! Talk with your child. Find out his or her feelings and make sure they matter to you. Learn to communicate early, and you will build a bridge that your child will be comfortable crossing throughout life.

How The Book Works *(cont.)*

How to Begin

As you have read in the previous pages, the areas of readiness are divided into the following four sections:

- Intellectual Readiness
- Physical Readiness
- Emotional Readiness
- Social Readiness

Overview and Checklist

Begin this book by reading the four readiness overviews and corresponding checklists. Then decide, based upon your child's needs, the area in which you would like to start. Remember, it is not necessary to begin at the beginning or move in sequential order through the book. The book is designed to work for your child, based on his or her specific needs.

Choose a Readiness Section

Look once again at the checklists for the corresponding readiness sections and determine where your child is today. Remember, there is no "place" that your child's abilities and skills should fall into on the checklist. They are provided as guides to help you get a sense of what a teacher might eventually expect of your child when he or she enters school.

Checklists for appropriate development are a baseline, or average, from which you (or later, a teacher) can determine the level of your child's current development in any area.

What Is Included in Each Section

You will notice that each section includes the following things:

1. An overview of the readiness area
2. A checklist of developmental milestones
3. A readiness story designed for you and your child to enjoy together
4. Developmentally appropriate activities that correspond to the milestones in the checklists and assist you in helping your child hone particular abilities and skills that are related to each area

How The Book Works (cont.)

How to Begin

Read the Story

Setting aside some time to look over the activities and read the stories will further help you determine where to begin. Then, enjoy the story with your child several times. Remember, it's a valuable part of reading readiness to read the same stories again and again to your child so that he or she can begin to recognize letters, words, and sequence of events.

Choose an Activity

Read over the activities that you are interested in and pick one. Notice that most of the activities in the book are designed to be repeated. In this way, you will be able to gauge over time your child's increased skills in a particular readiness area.

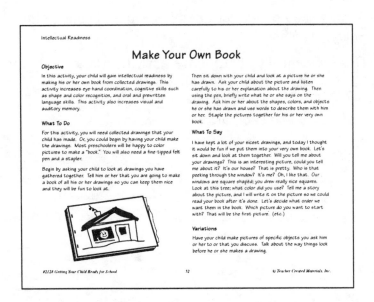

Milestone Checklist

Notice the Milestone Checklist pages. These pages are for you to make written observations of each activity after completing it with your child. The parent page reviews the areas of readiness that are highlighted in the activity and gives you specific ways to best observe each activity, based on the particular skill. Each Milestone Checklist looks like this:

As your child completes each activity for a second and third time, you will be able to review your comments from the previous attempt and notice the changes in his or her development.

From time to time, review the checklist for each section to help you make note of overall changes in your child's development.

Learning To Observe Your Child

The Art of Observation

"Learn to observe my child? I have been observing my child since she was born!" This may be true; however, you could still benefit by occasionally checking and improving your observation skills. These skills are important because in order to see your child more clearly, you must also examine your personal judgments, attitudes, and beliefs about parenting.

The following pages contain an observation activity that you can use to practice your observation skills. This activity will give you an opportunity to check your own observation skills and notice anything about yourself that will be helpful to be aware of while observing your child.

Observation Game

Aquarium Game

Week-Long Journal

Purpose:

This activity gives you the opportunity to do a long-term observation log or journal for five days and then repeat it again for five more days with slightly different rules. These activities are designed to help you learn how to observe your child in a nonjudgmental manner.

What You Need:

- Aquarium of fish to watch (a goldfish in a bowl will work, too)
- Journal Master (make as many copies as you need)
- Personal Journal Follow-up Form

What You Do:

Set aside 15 minutes every day to observe the aquarium (or fish bowl). Notice as much as possible on a daily basis, remembering to describe—but not judge—what you see in as complete a way as possible.

After a week's time, take a look at your entire log. See if you notice any patterns in what you recorded. Summarize what you saw. Did you begin to notice new and different things about the fish every day? If so, what were they? Did your written observations get longer in length, remain the same, or become shorter as the week progressed? All of these things could be important clues about keeping a journal or a log.

Try the same observation for another five days, except note each time before you begin how you feel and how your day is going. Do you feel tired, hurried, or anxious? Angry, annoyed, or frustrated? Happy and positive? Whatever kind of day you are having, make a note of it before you begin your observation.

At the end of the week, look again for patterns. Notice how possible it is to let emotions affect one's observations. Use these results to help you plan the best times to observe your child and to remain aware of how your own emotions could create a possible bias.

Journal—Five Days

Day One _____

Date _____ Time _____

Observations: _____

_____

_____

_____

_____

Day Two _____

Date _____ Time _____

Observations: _____

_____

_____

_____

Day Three _____

Date _____ Time _____

Observations: _____

_____

_____

_____

Day Four _____

Date _____ Time _____

Observations: _____

_____

_____

_____

Day Five _____

Date _____ Time _____

Observations: _____

_____

_____

Journal—Second Week

Day One _____

Date _____ Time _____

Observations: _____

_____

_____

_____

_____

_____

Day Two _____

Date _____ Time _____

Observations: _____

_____

_____

_____

_____

Day Three _____

Date _____ Time _____

Observations: _____

_____

_____

_____

_____

Day Four _____

Date _____ Time _____

Observations: _____

_____

_____

_____

_____

_____

Day Five _____

Date _____ Time _____

Observations: _____

_____

_____

_____

Personal Journal Follow-up Form

Look carefully at your second five days of observations. What do you notice? Do you see any patterns emerging? Do you see anything interesting about how you are feeling or what you have on your mind and how it affects your observations?

Possible Patterns

1. _____

   _____

   _____

2. _____

   _____

   _____

3. _____

   _____

   _____

4. _____

   _____

   _____

Notes:

It is possible that a "negative behavior" could have more to do with a parent's emotions than the subject's activity.

Share this activity with your spouse and compare your results.

Your response

_____

_____

_____

Spouse's response

_____

_____

_____

Now look carefully at your own emotional assessment section each day. How did these realizations about yourself and your feelings affect your own observation techniques and outcomes?

Inclusion and Assessment

What Is Full Inclusion?

Full inclusion is the term for including children with special needs into the regular classroom or early childhood setting. This practice is becoming more and more common today, and it is something that every parent should know about. It is important to understand the regular assessments that your child might be given, as well as regular procedures which children experience during a developmental screening. Through screening, it can be determined whether your child needs more thorough diagnostic assessment regarding a potential special need.

What Is Developmental Screening?

Developmental screening is a limited screening procedure to determine whether a child should have a diagnostic assessment. It is the first step in seeing if there is a potential problem that might require a child to have his or her needs met in a special way. This could be as simple as thinking a child might need glasses and contacting the parents about a free on-site vision test (which would be part of developmental screening). Or it could be as complicated as suspecting a variety of learning problems and getting the child the necessary developmental screening to determine whether diagnostic assessment (the second and more intensive step) is needed.

What Is Diagnostic Assessment?

Diagnostic assessment is the testing that determines a child's specific area of special needs. Through this testing, the best way of assisting the child through the use of special services and in compliance with legislation is determined.

What Steps Do I Take if I Think My Child Has Special Needs?

Many preschools and kindergartens take part in or refer students to a prekindergarten screening process of some kind. These developmental screening tests could test hearing and vision, motor skills, or a variety of other things. Find out what your child's new school's procedure is in this area. Here is a list of steps that you will need to take:

After your observation of your child, if you think your child might need to be screened for potential special needs, contact the school and discuss this with his or her new teacher.

Remember, you must give your written permission to have your child screened.

Remember that the tests that might be administered can vary, and different screening tools can produce different results. The goal of screening is to provide children with the best opportunity to learn and develop properly, not to label or exclude them in any way.

Find out what screening tools your child's school is using and make sure that these tools are reputable and proven.

Parent's Bill of Rights

- I have the right to select the school and educational environment that I think is best for my child.

- I have the right to make the final decision regarding my child's education.

- I have the right to meet with my child's teacher and voice any concerns I have about my child.

- I have the right to talk to a school administrator if I feel, after talking to a teacher, that my child's needs are not being met.

- I have the right to have my child tested and I can select an outside testing source at cost to me if I choose.

- I have the right to teach my child at home if I wish.

- I have the right to visit my child's classroom and observe.

- I have the right to insist that my child's special medical needs are met.

- I have the right to have my child assessed or evaluated for gifted and accelerated programs if I wish.

- I have the right to have my child enrolled in private or public school, depending on my preference.

Teacher's Bill of Rights

- Teachers have the right to be respected by parents, by children, and by administrators.

- Teachers have the right to be treated as professionals and acknowledged for their education, talents, and abilities with children.

- Teachers have the right to adequate pay for the work they do.

- Teachers have the right to assess the children they teach, make thoughtful observations, and plan in-class curriculum choices around the assessments they make.

- Teachers have the right to expect parents to work with them instead of against them.

- Teachers have the right to be treated with dignity.

- Teachers have the right to be acknowledged publicly for their contributions to the community.

- Teachers have the right to be told by parents about any special situations which affect their student while he or she is in the classroom.

- Teachers have the right to tell the truth in their classrooms.

Child's Bill of Rights

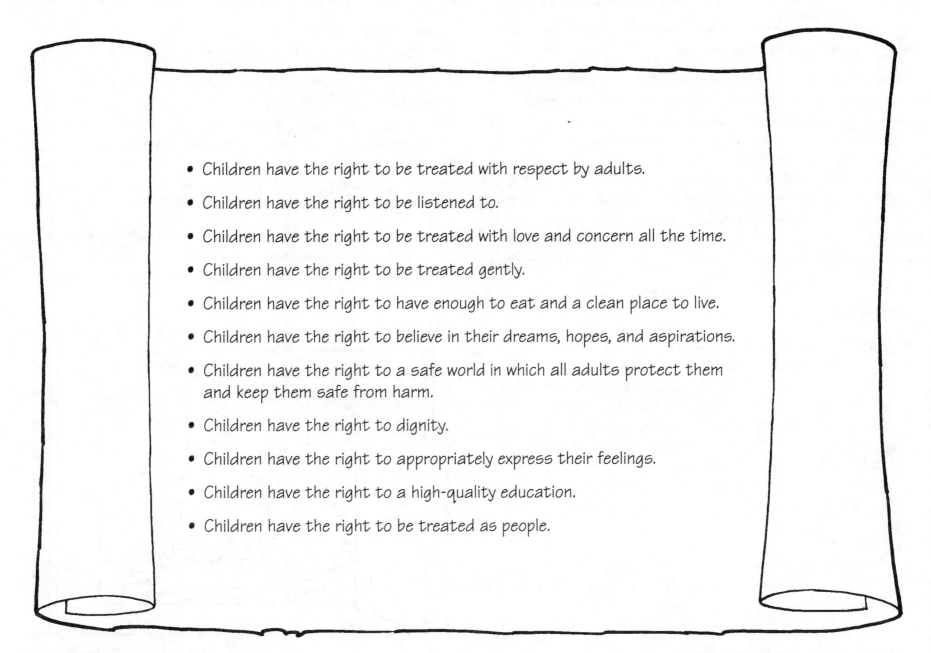

- Children have the right to be treated with respect by adults.

- Children have the right to be listened to.

- Children have the right to be treated with love and concern all the time.

- Children have the right to be treated gently.

- Children have the right to have enough to eat and a clean place to live.

- Children have the right to believe in their dreams, hopes, and aspirations.

- Children have the right to a safe world in which all adults protect them and keep them safe from harm.

- Children have the right to dignity.

- Children have the right to appropriately express their feelings.

- Children have the right to a high-quality education.

- Children have the right to be treated as people.

Intellectual Readiness Overview

What Is Intellectual Readiness?

Intellectual readiness concerns your child's appropriate level of mental development. As in all the other areas of readiness, there is quite a range of what is expected from young children and considered normal. Before entering school, your child will be expected to have the mental development necessary to learn the skills that are taught in the beginning curriculum. While some children come to their first day of school recognizing numbers, letters, and even words, many do not. We should give our children as much enrichment as possible, but remember that there could be extremes within the normal range of intellectual development.

Everyone Thinks

No matter what a child's abilities or skill level, we can enrich his or her environment. We can open the doors to the world for the child. We can give him or her many interesting and wonderful things to think about. We can ask his or her opinion. We can give him or her things to touch, to own, to play with, to use, to see, and to make. Most importantly, we can talk to the child. And, even more precious to him or her, we can learn to listen, and we can make sure that we do. This is the best way to enrich a child's life intellectually.

Different Children, Different Ways of Learning

As Dr. Howard Gardner, a noted Harvard scholar, has theorized, there are many different ways of being smart. Gone are the days when an IQ test totally determined one's fate. And luckily, with research and the dedication of high-level educators such as Dr. Gardner, our children have a world where the special people they are and the special talents and abilities they have may flourish.

The activities that follow in this section will help you help your child think. Use the checklist on the following page to determine your child's current level of intellectual readiness.

Intellectual Readiness Checklist

Reading Readiness

❑ Identifies and names the letters of the alphabet; likes to sing the alphabet song

❑ Identifies and says the sounds associated with the letters of the alphabet; names something that starts with each letter

❑ Identifies by sight and names words in his or her environment: e.g., "STOP" on a stop sign, his or her own name on a cubby, etc.

❑ Enjoys "reading" books by telling a story while looking at the pictures

Math Readiness

❑ Identifies and names the numerals from 1 to 10

❑ Counts ten objects; gives the number for a set of objects: e.g., 6 blocks, 2 bikes

❑ Forms the numerals from 1 to 10 using a variety of media: crayon, pencil, paint, clay, etc.

Writing Readiness

❑ Knows what the marks in books, on other papers, and on signs represent and can translate them into speech

❑ Enjoys dictating stories that are written down by the teacher or other classroom helper

❑ Forms the letters of the alphabet in a variety of media: crayon, pencil, paint, clay, etc

❑ Writes his or her own name

Science Readiness

❑ Sees the world as an amazing place full of interesting things to discover

❑ Looks and listens—spontaneously or as the result of directed activity—in order to find out about things

❑ Communicates with enthusiasm and some degree of accuracy what he or she finds out by observing things

I Think with My Brain

I have a brain inside of my head.

It works for me day and night without stopping.

I Think with My Brain (cont.)

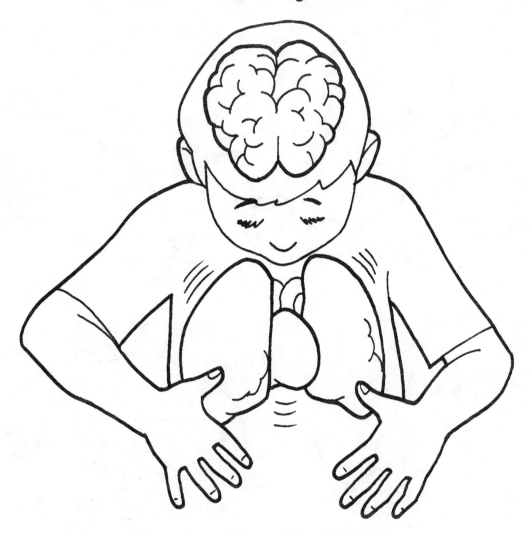

My brain does some things without being told.

It tells my heart to beat and my lungs to breathe.

I need not remind it to do those things.

I Think with My Brain (cont.)

When I want to move, my brain tells my muscles and bones what to do.

I don't have to learn things—like running or drawing—over again every time I do them.

My brain keeps track of how to do them for me.

I Think with My Brain (cont.)

When I sit down to eat, my brain says "Yummy!" or "Yucky!"

It tells me when I'm hungry and when my stomach is full.

It says "Drink some water!" when I am hot and thirsty.

I Think with My Brain *(cont.)*

When I open my eyes, my brain looks at things.

It can see my friend who lives way down the street.

It can see the words in a book.

It can tell me what colors I'm looking at.

24

I Think with My Brain (cont.)

My brain can tell me about the sounds my ears hear.

It can listen to people when they talk and when they play music.

I Think with My Brain (cont.)

After I tell my brain the rules, it remembers them for me.

It reminds me by yelling, "No!" or "Don't go!" inside my head.

I Think with My Brain (cont.)

My brain can learn things.

It can learn the ABC's and how to count by two's.

It can learn where China is and what the moon is made of.

I Think with My Brain (cont.)

My brain can remember things.

It can remember the animals I saw at the zoo.

It can remember what I got for my last birthday.

I Think with My Brain (cont.)

My brain can think of ideas.

It can think up songs to sing and secrets to tell.

It can think up the beginning, middle, and end of a story.

I Think with My Brain (cont.)

My brain can take all of the ideas I have and connect them in new ways.

Just as my body gets stronger when I exercise, my brain gets stronger when I think.

Every time I use my brain, it gets stronger.

I Think with My Brain (cont.)

I like to learn about my brain.

The more I know about it, the better it works.

"Once Upon a Time" Stories

Objective

In this activity your child will gain intellectual readiness by not only adding to oral stories you create but create his or her own as well. This activity encourages oral language skills, language comprehension, memory, sequencing, creativity, and comprehension.

What To Do

Begin by reading your child a story. This could be either your favorite or a new story for your child. After you have completed this, ask your child if he or she would like to hear a story you will make up. Most children will not refuse such a treat!

Begin the story with "Once upon a time . . . ," and then tell a simple story that includes you and your child in a pretend or real situation. Be sure to tell your child ahead of time if you

are going to tell a story about something that really happened, is going to happen, or one that is just pretend. Just before you get to the end of the story, ask your child what he or she thinks will happen and ask him or her to help make up the ending.

Try this a number of times until your child is comfortable enough and then ask him or her to tell you a story. This could be done on a regular basis and is a great way to pass a few spare minutes or as a bedtime story alternative.

What To Say

Now that I've read you your favorite book, I want to tell you a story that isn't written down. Ready? This is going to be a real story about something we did yesterday. When I get to the end, you can help me.

Once upon a time there was a mommy and a little girl named Sara. Sara and her mommy loved to bake cookies, so one day they decided to make peanut butter cookies. First they read the recipe, then they got all of the ingredients, and finally they mixed the cookies. What happened next? (At this point let your child finish the story or assist him or her in finishing it.)

Variations

Have your child tell you a bedtime story. Ask him or her to tell you a story about a family member or a friend or ask him or her to tell a story about something he or she would like to do in the future.

"Once Upon a Time" Stories (cont.)

Milestone Checklist

❑ My child could predict the ending of a simple story.

❑ My child could end a story I began.

❑ My child could make up and tell a simple story.

❑ What was the subject of our first story? _____

Did my child supply an ending?   Yes ❑   No ❑

Describe the ending briefly for your own reference:

_____

_____

_____

_____

What did I notice the first time I asked my child to finish a story?

_____

_____

_____

_____

_____

Activity Repetitions

#2

❑ I told the story and my child guessed the ending.

❑ I told the story and my child finished it.

❑ My child told the following story:

_____

_____

_____

#3

❑ I told the story and my child guessed the ending.

❑ I told the story and my child finished it.

❑ My child told the following story:

_____

_____

_____

Grocery Clerk Game

Objective

In this activity your child will gain intellectual readiness by pretending to be a grocery clerk and storing groceries in your kitchen. This activity enhances intellectual readiness by reinforcing many skills, including sorting and classifying skills, counting, ordering, and sequencing. This activity also enhances language comprehension.

What To Do

Begin this activity after having completed your grocery shopping, or take canned and other nonperishable goods out of your pantry to play grocery clerk. Let your child take the items out of the grocery bag and talk with him or her about what they are. Use the words to name each and talk about what one makes with them as well as how many there are, whether they are big or little, hard or soft, etc.

As your child removes the items, suggest that you count them together. Classify items with your child. For example, help him or her put all the canned goods in one place and the cereal boxes in another, the small things in one place and the larger things in another. There are a variety of different ways you could sort and classify groceries, and all of them are useful in this activity.

What To Say

Will you help me put the groceries away? I need help sorting everything we bought and making sure I put everything in the best place. I want to count the things we bought. Let's start with these apples. Could you help me count them? One, two, three, four, five, and six. Okay, we have six apples. Now let's look at the boxes of cereal. We don't have many of these, do we? There are how many? One, and here is another. That is two. Now let's find all the little things and put them over here on the counter so we don't lose them. The gum is little. And the candy bar is little. This bag of potato chips is really big.

Variations

Have your child pick the biggest item in a group. Separate the groceries by his or her favorite and least favorite items or by color, texture, or shape.

Grocery Clerk Game (cont.)

Milestone Checklist

❑ My child could sort items by size
on_____/_____/_____.

❑ My child could sort items by color
on_____/_____/_____.

❑ My child could group things by type
on_____/_____/_____.

❑ My child could count from one to ten
on_____/_____/_____.

❑ My child could count from one to twenty
on_____/_____/_____.

❑ My child recognizes letter symbols
on_____/_____/_____.

❑ What was your child's reaction to being invited to play "grocery clerk"?

_____

What items did your child recognize and name?

_____ _____ _____

_____ _____ _____

_____ _____ _____

_____ _____ _____

Did your child understand the difference between
"big and little"? _____

"hard and soft"? _____

What colors could he or she name?

_____

What were your other observations about the activity?

_____

_____

Activity Repetitions

#1

❑ My child recognized and named items.

❑ My child recognized letters or words.

❑ My child counted from_____to_____.

Other observations:

_____

_____

#2

❑ My child recognized and named items.

❑ My child recognized letters or words.

❑ My child counted from_____to_____.

Other observations:

_____

_____

Eat My ABC's

Objective

In this activity your child will gain intellectual readiness by helping to make his or her own morning cereal and becoming familiar with the alphabet. This activity enhances your child's letter recognition, which later will set the stage for reading readiness. Oral language skills and small muscle skills are respectively enhanced as your child names letters and manipulates small objects.

What To Do

Begin this activity by inviting your preschooler to eat an alphabet cereal for breakfast. Start out by letting your child pour cereal into a bowl and look at the cereal before actually pouring on milk. (After your child is done looking at the ABC cereal is the best time to pour on the milk. Prior to this there is always the chance he will reach into the bowl and pull out soggy letters!)

With your child, look through the letters in the bowl and see which he recognizes. If your child doesn't know any letters by sight, begin by taking out an "A" and telling him or her the name of the letter. Do this on a regular basis until he begins to recognize the letters himself.

After he begins to recognize the letters, ask him to find letters at random or more than one of the same letter. Then show your child how to spell his or her name with alphabet cereal. See how many simple words you can teach your child using this method.

What To Say

I bought us a special kind of cereal that has ABC shapes. Let's take a look at all the letters before we eat breakfast. Do you know the names of any of these letters? This one is an "A." Let's try to find another "A." And here is the letter "B." Let's see if we can find "C." We can do this a lot until we find the whole alphabet.

Variations

As you and your child are exploring the alphabet cereal, sing the alphabet song or talk about the different things that start with each letter. Pick a letter each day and see how many things you find on your way to preschool or on errands that begin with that letter.

Eat My ABC's *(cont.)*

Milestone Checklist

- ❑ My child knew five to ten alphabet letters on_____/_____/_____.
- ❑ My child could say the ABC's on_____/_____/_____.
- ❑ My child could tell the difference between a B and a P on_____/_____/_____.
- ❑ My child could tell the difference between an E and an F on_____/_____/_____.
- ❑ My child could sing the ABC song on_____/_____/_____.
- ❑ My child could move ABC letters into order on_____/_____/_____.

What letters does my child recognize today?

_____   _____   _____

_____   _____   _____

_____   _____   _____

_____   _____   _____

I pointed out the following letters and said their names:

_____

_____

I showed my child how to spell his or her name and he could:

name the letters on_____/_____/_____.

match the letters on_____/_____/_____.

do it alone after me_____/_____/_____.

I sang the ABC song for my child and he or she:

listened on_____/_____/_____.

sang some of the words on_____/_____/_____.

sang all of the words on_____/_____/_____.

Activity Repetitions

#2

- ❑ My child recognized these letters: _____
Other observations: _____

_____

#3

- ❑ My child recognized these letters: _____
Other observations: _____

_____

"What Is This?" Game

Objective

In this activity, your child will gain intellectual readiness by exploring the world around him or her and learning the names of objects, places, and things. This activity increases language comprehension, cognitive thinking, and oral language skills.

What To Do

This game is a simple one that could be frequently repeated to increase your child's understanding of the world around him or her.

Begin by noticing the world around you. All too often, as harried parents we forget to notice our environment, and in doing so our children don't receive the benefit of our responses to the things we see.

During the course of a day at home, or in your travels around town with your child, use the time to talk to one another. Ask your child what he or she thinks of what is seen, to name this or that, to tell you what is noticed. It's vitally important for language development that people are actually spoken to and listened to. If your child asks a question and you provide a disjointed or unrelated answer, the result could be confusion about what words and messages mean.

This activity will not only increase your child's language comprehension and concrete thinking, but also serve as a training ground for increased lifelong communication between the two of you.

What To Say

I noticed that the clock over there is very tall. Do you know what that kind of clock is called? It's a grandfather's clock. What else do you notice about the clock? Let's see what other kinds of clocks we could see today while we walk around town.

Variation

As you play this game with your child, you will probably find yourself making up special games that you always play together. You may, for example, always look for red cars or pay attention to especially pretty trees, flowers or animals. Anything, and any topic, will work for this activity.

"What Is This?" Game (cont.)

Milestone Checklist

- ❑ My child knew the names of common animals
  on_____/_____/_____.
- ❑ My child could name the colors on_____/_____/_____.
- ❑ My child could name common articles of clothing
  on_____/_____/_____.
- ❑ My child could name common objects in the house
  on_____/_____/_____.
- ❑ My child could name common objects outside
  on_____/_____/_____.

What my child noticed today:

_____

What I explained to my child today:

_____

New words, experiences, or ideas I have noticed my child sharing:

_____

_____

Other observations:

_____

_____

Activity Repetitions

#2

What did we talk about today?

_____

_____

_____

What new things did my child share today?

_____

_____

_____

#3

What did we talk about today?

_____

_____

_____

What new things did my child share today?

_____

_____

_____

How Big Am I?

Objective

In this activity, your child gains intellectual readiness by learning about shapes, sizes, weight, and other measurement through relevant, real-life experiences. This activity exposes children to intuitive and concrete thinking skills and experiences, estimation, logic, premath and science, and linear thinking.

What To Do

Begin this activity by buying or creating a measuring wall chart to gauge your child's height. This could be as elaborate as a purchased measuring wall hanging or as simple as having your child lean against an inconspicuous door jamb, measuring and marking the height with a pencil. Additionally, you will need a bathroom scale so that your child can chart his or her weight.

Preschoolers are very interested in the fact that they are growing. This is directly related to their own sense of mastery and self. While you are sharing the experience of weighing and measuring your child, be sure to comment positively about how wonderful it is that he or she is growing so big and strong.

Talk with your child about how many pounds he or she weighs and how many inches he or she measures. You could repeat this process monthly and — though it only takes a few minutes — you will be reinforcing important skills and concepts with your child.

What To Say

You are looking awfully grown-up today! We should measure you and weigh you and see if you have grown. Would you like to do that? We could make a little chart and make a tiny mark on the wall in my bathroom so we could see how much you are growing every month. Let's try it. Let's see. Step on the bathroom scale. You weigh 42 pounds! That is one pound more than last time. And you are 42 inches too. That is three-and-a half feet. Wow, I'm impressed! I bet you are tall enough to go on new rides at the amusement park.

Variations

Make a simple paper chart with your child and keep a record of his or her weight and height.

How Big Am I? *(cont.)*

Milestone Checklist

☐ My child knew his or her weight on_____/_____/_____.

☐ My child knew his or her height on_____/_____/_____.

☐ My child could classify objects as big, bigger, biggest on_____/_____/_____.

☐ My child could classify objects as little, littler, littlest on_____/_____/_____.

☐ My child knew inches and feet are related to height on_____/_____/_____.

☐ My child knew that pounds are related to weight on_____/_____/_____.

The first time I weighed and measured my child, we talked about the following:

_____

_____

_____

The following terms were new to my child:

_____ _____ _____

_____ _____ _____

_____ _____ _____

_____ _____ _____

My child was familiar with these things:

_____

_____

Other observations:

_____

_____

My child's height and weight today are _____.

Activity Repetitions

#2

My child's height and weight today are _____.

Repeating the activity, I observed this about my child:

_____

_____

#3

My child's height and weight today are _____.

Repeating the activity, I observed this about my child:

_____

_____

Shopping List Game

Objective

In this activity, your child will gain intellectual readiness by exposure to numbers, words, and meanings by seeing the corresponding tangible objects. This activity increases language comprehension, number and word recognition, sequencing, logic, and comparison. These are important prereading and premath skills.

What To Do

This activity could be completed any time you are going shopping at any store when a list might be handy.

Begin this activity by telling your child you need his or her help making a shopping list. Then talk with your child about what you need at the store. Begin listing items. Print each legibly on a piece of paper. Then point at the written word and say it aloud.

When you arrive at the store, read the list item by item, pointing to the word again as you read it. Then, find the item, and point out an important or interesting feature and place it in your cart. Draw a line through the item and count the remainder. Keep going until you have found everything.

What To Say

I need you to help me make a grocery list. Let's get a clean piece of paper and a pen. Now, help me think of what we need. Do we need fruit? What kind? I think we need apples. How many do you think we should get? Okay, six apples. How about bread? I know we need bread. We need it to make lunches this week, so how many loaves shall we get? Two.

Once at the store, say "First, apples. See it here on our list. This word is the word "apples." Let's find them. Now, we wrote a number six by the apples. What was that for? Oh yes, we need six. Will you help me count them? Thank you."

Variations

As your child shops regularly, you will notice his or her skill in helping you will increase. As your child begins to recognize and write words, let him or her do more.

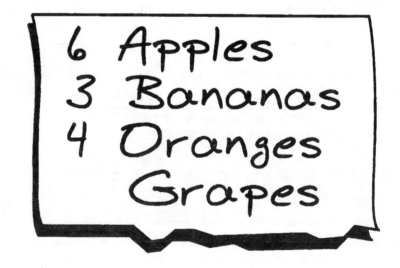

Shopping List Game (cont.)

Milestone Checklist

- ☐ My child recognized the alphabet
  on_____/_____/_____.
- ☐ My child recognized the numbers 1–10
  on_____/_____/_____.
- ☐ My child made logical choices for the grocery list
  on_____/_____/_____.
- ☐ My child recognized words on the grocery list
  on_____/_____/_____.

First Shopping List:

_____

_____

_____

_____

Observations:

_____

_____

_____

_____

_____

Activity Repetitions

#2

How did our list-making change the second time?

_____

_____

_____

My child's word usage and understanding increased in the following way:

_____

_____

_____

#3

How did our list-making change the third time?

_____

_____

_____

My child's word usage and understanding increased in the following way:

_____

_____

_____

Family Letter

Objective

In this activity, your child will gain intellectual readiness by receiving and, eventually, writing notes with your help. This activity increases letter and word recognition, oral and written communication skills, and comprehension of language.

What To Do

This note-writing activity should be used regularly as a part of actual communication between you and your child. Besides the obvious readiness benefits of communication, your child will be glad that you care enough to write to him or her and will treasure many notes that the two of you share.

Begin by printing your child a simple and legible note to leave somewhere in the house. Draw his or her attention to it. A good time for this may be when you are leaving your child with a sitter or any other time you want to share something in writing. A simple note that says "Mommy will be home later. Be good for Grandma." is an excellent start. Grandma, another adult, or even an older sibling could help your child read the note.

What To Say

I am going out for a little while, and I have left a note for you. Grandma could read it to you. Maybe you and Grandma could write a note back to me sometime while I am gone. That would make me very happy.

Variations

Ask your child to draw you a picture note in response to your note. Or leave a simple note on the refrigerator or on his or her bedroom door.

Family Letter (cont.)

Milestone Checklist

❑ My child listened to a letter being read to him or her
on_____/_____/_____.

❑ My child took an interest in writing his or her own
letter on_____/_____/_____.

❑ My child used "pretend cursive" to "write" a letter
on_____/_____/_____.

❑ My child recognized the letters in the alphabet
on_____/_____/_____.

❑ My child understood the message in a short letter
read on_____/_____/_____.

❑ My child wrote letters on_____/_____/_____.

❑ My child wrote a word on_____/_____/_____.

The first letter I wrote to my child said the following:

_____

_____

_____

My child reacted this way:

_____

_____

_____

My child's first dictated letter to me read:

_____

_____

_____

My Child's First Letter:

_____

_____

Activity Repetition Notes:

_____

_____

_____

What Happened First?

Objective

In this activity your child will gain intellectual readiness through logic, sequencing, and memory. This activity will help increase your child's school readiness by focusing on skills that will later be used in mathematics, reading, and science.

What To Do

Begin this activity any time you have a few minutes to talk to your child. This activity can work with you and your child alone, but it also is a natural activity to introduce when a third interested party is involved.

The idea behind this activity is to give your child an opportunity to think about events that happened and recall the order or sequence in which they did. Remember, recall and sequencing are processes that are mastered over a number of years. However, practicing these skills will only increase them, and that is positive, no matter what your child's level of mastery is. (Just think about what you ate for breakfast three days ago — and the order in which you ate it—if you are concerned that you child isn't excelling at this sort of memory sequencing!)

Ask your child about an event that happened earlier in the day. For example, you might ask what he or she liked best about breakfast, or what he or she liked about a favorite program watched earlier in the day. Help him or her construct his or her answers, making sure to ask him or her things that you know about. Be positive and nonjudgmental about his or her replies.

What To Say

What did you watch on TV this morning? What characters did you see? What did they do? What was your favorite part?

Variation

Ask your child to share a memory with a friend or family member. These responses will help your child with the skills associated with the activity as well as communication skills.

What Happened First? *(cont.)*

Milestone Checklist

- ☐ My child remembered what happened earlier in the day on_____/_____/_____.
- ☐ My child could recall the order of two events on_____/_____/_____.
- ☐ My child could tell about a story he or she just heard on_____/_____/_____.
- ☐ My child recalled what happens in the morning each day on_____/_____/_____.
- ☐ My child remembered some facts about a short TV show on_____/_____/_____.

The first event my child recalled was

_____

_____

_____

I noticed this about his or her ability to recall what happened:

_____

_____

_____

_____

Activity Repetitions

#2

My child recalled the following event:

_____

_____

_____

Observations and comparisons:

_____

_____

_____

#3

My child recalled the following event:

_____

_____

_____

Observations and comparisons:

_____

_____

_____

Kitchen Measuring Game

Objective

In this activity, your child will increase his or her thinking skills. This activity provides exposure to the concepts of opposites: big and little, more and less, empty and full, fast and slow. These concepts will set the stage for later learning in science and mathematics.

What To Do

This activity could be used anytime you are in the kitchen preparing a meal. It works very well with a recipe for which you might need to measure ingredients. Or just get out some measuring spoons, cups, some dry cereal, and a pitcher for water.

Begin this activity by asking your child to help you in the kitchen. Read over a recipe with your child and let him or her help measure the ingredients. Talk about what you are doing and use the words "big" and "little," "more" and "less," "empty" and "full," etc. Talk about how long it takes you to make a recipe. Does it take a long time or a short time? Look at the clock and talk about what your child believes is a long time— you might be very surprised!

What To Say

Would you like to help me make cookies? Let's wash our hands, and we can try it. First, let's look at the ingredients. We are going to use flour. We are going to measure it in a measuring cup. We need two cups. Let's fill this cup up until it's full. Let's pour it into a bowl. Now our bowl is nearly full, and the cup is empty. Let's try the same thing with the sugar. . . .

Variations

Let your child measure water or dry cereal as an activity that doesn't involve food preparation. Or take some plastic measuring cups and spoons in the bathroom for tub toys. Talk about the concepts while your child has a bath as an alternative to kitchen measuring.

Kitchen Measuring Game (cont.)

Milestone Checklist

❑ My child understood the concept of "big and little" on_____/_____/_____.

❑ My child understood the concept of "fast and slow" on_____/_____/_____.

❑ My child understood the concept of "empty and full" on_____/_____/_____.

❑ My child could manipulate a measuring cup and spoon on_____/_____/_____.

❑ My child could follow one simple measuring direction on_____/_____/_____.

❑ My child could follow two simple measuring directions on_____/_____/_____.

Our first kitchen experience was: _____

From the Kitchen of . . . _____

How my child felt about the kitchen experience:

_____

_____

My child understood these ideas:

_____

_____

I want to stress these ideas next time:

_____

_____

Activity Repetitions

#2

How my child felt about the kitchen experience:

_____

_____

My child understood these ideas:

_____

_____

I want to stress these ideas next time:

_____

_____

#3

How my child felt about the kitchen experience:

_____

_____

My child understood these ideas:

_____

_____

I want to stress these ideas next time:

_____

_____

Picture Stories

Objective

In this activity, your child will gain intellectual readiness by looking at several pictures and discussing an event that occurred. This activity fosters cognitive skills such as the ability to think visually, make visual distinctions, and the ability to communicate orally.

What To Do

Although preschoolers tend to be concrete, they also use "magical thinking" which is intuitive rather than logical. This is normal and expected. Don't expect your child to start out mastering this activity. Remember it's a gradual process.

Begin this activity by gathering pictures from magazines or newspapers. Another interesting choice would be family photographs of events such as parties or travel in which your child participated.

Ask your child to tell what happened in each picture, or if it's a family photograph, ask your child to recall an event. If it's a picture from a book or magazine, your child will need to find the correct words to describe the picture.

Give your child help as needed, as well as information about things he or she doesn't know about. Ask open-ended questions when appropriate to encourage a more complete verbal response.

What To Say

Let's look at the pictures I just got back from our vacation to St. Louis. Remember this? What is this big building? Yes, its the Arch. What did you like about it? Yes, I liked going up inside it, too. What do you remember about that day?

Variations

When you are reading a storybook to your child, before turning the page at an exciting moment, ask him or her what will happen next. Then listen to the response and continue the story. Discuss his or her thoughts and compare them to what actually happened.

Picture Stories (cont.)

Milestone Checklist

❑ My child named the object in a simple picture
on_____/_____/_____.

❑ My child named 2–5 objects in a picture
on_____/_____/_____.

❑ My child explained what is happening in a simple picture
on_____/_____/_____.

❑ My child recognized familiar people from photographs
on_____/_____/_____.

❑ My child recognized familiar places from photographs
on_____/_____/_____.

My child and I looked at these illustrations:

_____

_____

and these photographs:

_____

_____

My child named these objects, places or people:

_____   _____   _____

_____   _____   _____

I explained this:

_____

_____

_____

Activity Repetitions:

#2

My child looked at these pictures:

_____

_____

_____

She or he named, described or discussed the following:

_____

_____

_____

#3

My child looked at these pictures:

_____

_____

_____

She or he named, described or discussed the following:

_____

_____

_____

Make Your Own Book

Objective

In this activity, your child will gain intellectual readiness by making his or her own book from collected drawings. This activity increases eye-hand coordination, cognitive skills such as shape and color recognition, and oral and prewritten language skills. This activity also increases visual and auditory memory.

What To Do

For this activity, you will need collected drawings that your child has made. Or, you could begin by having your child make the drawings. Most preschoolers will be happy to color pictures to make a "book." You will also need a fine-tipped felt pen and a stapler.

Begin by asking your child to look at drawings you have gathered together. Tell him or her that you are going to make a book of all his or her drawings so you can keep them nice and they will be fun to look at.

Then sit down with your child and look at a picture he or she has drawn. Ask your child about the picture and listen carefully to his or her explanation about the drawing. Then using the pen, briefly write what he or she says on the drawing. Ask him or her about the shapes, colors, and objects he or she has drawn and use words to describe them with him or her. Staple the pictures together for his or her very own book.

What To Say

I have kept a lot of your nicest drawings, and today I thought it would be fun if we put them into your very own book. Let's sit down and look at them together. Will you tell me about your drawings? This is an interesting picture, could you tell me about it? It's our house? That is pretty. Who is that peeking through the window? It's me? Oh, I like that. Our windows are square shaped; you drew really nice squares. Look at this tree; what color did you use? Tell me a story about the picture, and I will write it on the picture so we could read your book after it's done. Let's decide what order we want them in the book. Which picture do you want to start with? That will be the first picture. (etc.)

Variations

Have your child make pictures of specific objects you ask him or her to or that you discuss. Talk about the way things look before he or she makes a drawing.

Make Your Own Book (cont.)

My Very Own Book

Milestone Checklist

❑ My child could easily hold crayons
on_____/_____/_____.

❑ My child could draw faces and stick figures
on_____/_____/_____.

❑ My child drew pictures with several objects
on_____/_____/_____.

❑ My child could explain his or her drawing to me
on_____/_____/_____.

My child's first "book title" was:

_____

_____

I noticed this about my child's drawings today:

_____

_____

I noticed my child is drawing the following objects:

_____

_____

I noticed these changes in my child's small motor skills:

_____

_____

Activity Repetition

#2

I noticed this about my child's drawings today:

_____

_____

I noticed my child is drawing the following objects:

_____

_____

I noticed these changes in my child's small motor skills:

_____

_____

#3

I noticed this about my child's drawings today:

_____

_____

I noticed my child is drawing the following objects:

_____

_____

I noticed these changes in my child's small motor skills:

_____

_____

Physical Readiness Overview

What Is Physical Readiness?

Physical readiness is your child's appropriate level of physical maturity based on his or her individual development. Experts agree that there is an expected range of physical development and ability for children of differing age levels and that by the time your child enters school, he or she will be expected to meet the normal range in basic physical behaviors. However, just as children walk at different ages, they also achieve every other kind of physical milestone at their own particular moment in time.

Everyone Moves

Children love to use their large muscles. They love to play. They walk, run, hop, skip, and use tricycles and toys. They dance, clap their hands, and march in time to music. They may attempt all kinds of energetic and sometimes dangerous physical maneuvers and need to be cautioned, taught safety rules, and be carefully supervised. Most of all, they need to be provided with truly safe places to play—places with soft surfaces and strong equipment with a smooth finish.

Children love to use their small muscles, too. They love to color, draw, and work with tools. They attack their buttons, zippers, and laces with an enthusiasm that could, and often does, turn to frustration. They need lots of opportunities to practice and just the right amount of help to get over the rough spots. Most of all, they need understanding and reassurance.

Different Children, Different Bodies

The fact that children love to do physical activities doesn't mean they will all do them at the same age. Some children are naturally strong and coordinated; some are not. Some differently-abled children will have to work toward skills and abilities that most children develop naturally. But that doesn't mean that children with physical challenges can't enjoy movement. They will be faced with harder work and more frustration, as will their parents, but they can still take pleasure from the things they are able to do, especially if each success is celebrated and enjoyed.

The activities that follow in this section will help your child move. Use the checklist on the following page to determine your child's current level of physical readiness.

54

Physical Readiness Checklist

Large Motor Skills

❑ Uses and enjoys physical skills such as walking, running, and jumping

❑ Accelerates and decelerates easily while running, could make sudden stops and turn sharp corners

❑ Has a well-developed sense of equilibrium and can hop, skip, jump upward, and balance on one foot momentarily

❑ Uses alternating foot pattern for stairs; can pedal a tricycle or bike.

❑ Throws, catches, and bounces a ball with increasing success

❑ Puts on and takes off his or her own clothes

Psychomotor Skills

❑ Has auditory discrimination, e.g., follows verbal directions

❑ Has visual discrimination, e.g., dodges a moving ball

❑ Has kinesthetic discrimination, e.g., makes bodily adjustments to maintain balance

❑ Has tactile discrimination, e.g., determines texture through touch

❑ Has coordination skills, e.g., jumps rope, kicks a ball, plays jacks, plays video games

Small Motor Skills

❑ Manipulates buttons, snaps, zippers, and shoelaces, but may not yet tie a bow

❑ Uses eating utensils—fork and spoon—easily; uses blunt, dull knife for spreading

❑ Fits together jigsaw puzzles and enjoys other games that demand dexterity

❑ Draws, writes, colors, etc. with increasing precision and ease

❑ Uses scissors with increasing skill and precision

❑ Uses a computer keyboard and/or mouse with confidence

Too Little, Too Big!

Daisy was a little girl, only four years old.

After all, her mother thought she was little.

She even called Daisy "baby."

Too Little, Too Big! (cont.)

Her uncle thought she was little, too.

Granny thought she was little, too.

After all, Granny warned Daisy that she was too small

to reach the top shelves and told her never to climb

on the kitchen counter.

Too Little, Too Big! (cont.)

But Daisy was big. She was sure of it.

After all, she grew every year on her birthday, overnight, like magic, didn't she?

And she had had four birthdays. She was grown up!

Too Little, Too Big! *(cont.)*

That is why Daisy got very upset when she didn't know how to do something or when her mommy told her she couldn't do something because she said Daisy was too little.

#2128 Getting Your Child Ready for School

Too Little, Too Big! (cont.)

Then, at other times, her mommy wouldn't let Daisy

do something because she said she was too big!

Sometimes Daisy felt like yelling. "Too little! Too big!

Which is it? What am I? Little? Or big?"

60

Too Little, Too Big! (cont.)

Daisy knew she was big enough to sit at the dinner table
and eat with the family. But much of the time she would rather eat in
the family room and watch tapes on the TV.

Too Little, Too Big! (cont.)

Daisy knew she was big enough to dress herself.

But sometimes a zipper would get stuck

or a shoe wouldn't lace, and Daisy would cry.

Too Little, Too Big! (cont.)

MUST BE TALLER THAN THIS

Even though Daisy didn't get scared on the scary rides

at the amusement park, she still wasn't tall enough to ride the best rides.

Did that make her little? Or big?

#2128 Getting Your Child Ready for School

Too Little, Too Big! (cont.)

Daisy was big enough to spread her peanut butter on bread

with a dull knife. But sometimes her mommy

wouldn't let her in the kitchen, saying "You're too little."

Too Little, Too Big! (cont.)

Daisy was big enough to sleep in her own bed.

But sometimes it was still more fun to cuddle in bed with her parents.

#2128 Getting Your Child Ready for School

Too Little, Too Big! (cont.)

Sometimes she felt little, but people wanted her to do some things for herself. Then she would feel big, but people would step in and do things for her. Then Daisy got an idea . . . .

Too Little, Too Big! *(cont.)*

She went into her parents' bedroom to look in the mirror.

Yes, that was it—she was somewhere in the middle.

She wasn't big. She wasn't little, but she was the perfect size for a four-year-old.

"I know what I am!" Daisy said "I'm just right."

And she was.

Family Place Cards

Objective

In this activity, your child will gain physical readiness by making family place cards for dinner or other occasions. This activity increases oral and written language skills, reading readiness, and premath skills by providing exposure to letters, words, and shapes. Additionally, your child's small motor skills and eye-hand coordination will increase as he or she manipulates objects and uses small tools.

What To Do

Use this activity any time you want to involve your child in a holiday meal, or just for fun for any meal.

Begin by gathering together crayons, glue, construction paper, a felt pen, and safety scissors. Fold the construction paper in half and in half again to create a standing card. Next, help your child list who needs a place card and where you each should sit. Help your child decorate the cards and write people's names. Place cards could be made for any occasion, and many simple shapes will do. For example, cut out orange circles and green rectangle stems to glue on the cards for Halloween pumpkins. Cut out green triangles to glue on cards for winter holidays. Talk with your child about his or her ideas and assist with the execution. Your child will be proud of his or her contribution to the event, and everyone will love the place cards!

What To Say

Let's make place cards for the table for Halloween. Won't that be fun? We can cut out pumpkins and decorate them. Pumpkins will be easy. We can make circles, and we can use tiny rectangles of green paper for their stems. Let's try it!

Variations

Use the same idea to let your child create homemade greeting cards. Talk about the letters in each person's name and how you spell them or write each name for your child to copy.

Family Place Cards (cont.)

Milestone Checklist

❑ My child could draw circles and squares
  on_____/_____/_____.

❑ My child used safety scissors with some success
  on_____/_____/_____.

❑ My child followed a simple direction
  on_____/_____/_____.

❑ My child recognized the letters and could name them
  on_____/_____/_____.

❑ My child could fold a piece of paper in half
  on_____/_____/_____.

❑ My child could recognize his or her name
  on_____/_____/_____.

We chose to make place cards for the following occasion:

_____

My child made place cards for the following people:

_____ _____ _____

_____ _____ _____

I noticed the following about how my child followed simple directions:

_____

I noticed the following about how my child manipulated a pen, crayon, and scissors:

_____

Activity Repetitions

#2

I noticed the following about how my child followed simple directions:

_____

I noticed this about how my child manipulated a pen, crayon, and scissors:

_____

Overall impressions:

_____

#3

I noticed the following about how my child followed simple directions:

_____

I noticed this about how my child manipulated a pen, crayon, and scissors:

_____

Overall impressions:

_____

"I Am an Animal" Game

Objective

In this activity your child increases language skills while building comprehension of the world around him. He will become increasingly familiar with animals and the noises they make while using large motor skills and coordination. This activity also increases prescience skills and auditory memory.

What To Do

This animal mimicry activity can take several forms, depending on whether you will be able to join your child on the ground to play, or you need to play using only your voices and imaginations.

Begin this activity by talking about an animal you are thinking of. Give hints or clues about the animal. With preschoolers you will have to be very obvious. Give your child the kind of hints that will make it possible to guess the animal and win the game. Then ask your child to be the animal. This gives your child a chance to be creative and physical, and engage in the playacting and pretending that are necessary and important to young children.

What To Say

I am thinking of an animal. This is an animal that people have in their houses and keep as pets. It goes like this: "Meow, meow." Could you tell me the animal's name? That's right! It is a cat. Let's pretend we are cats.

I am thinking of an animal. This is an animal in a zoo or in Africa. The animal is dangerous. It makes a loud noise like this: "Roar!" Do you know the name of this animal? That's right! It is a lion. Let's pretend we are lions and roar!

Variations

As your child's comprehension increases, make the clues a little more difficult. Begin with hard clues and then make the clues easier, as necessary.

"I Am an Animal" Game *(cont.)*

Milestone Checklist

My child knows the names of the following animals:

- ❑ Cat
- ❑ Dog
- ❑ Bird
- ❑ Mouse
- ❑ Lion
- ❑ Sheep

- ❑ Pig
- ❑ Horse
- ❑ Goat
- ❑ Deer
- ❑ Rabbit
- ❑ Cow

- ❑ Giraffe
- ❑ Zebra
- ❑ Monkey

Others: _____

_____

_____

_____

My child guessed the following animals today:

_____   _____   _____

_____   _____   _____

My child could make sounds for the following animals today:

_____   _____   _____

_____   _____   _____

My child could imitate the following animals today:

_____   _____   _____

_____   _____   _____

Activity Repetitions

#2

My child guessed the following animals today:

_____   _____   _____

_____   _____   _____

My child could make sounds for the following animals today:

_____   _____   _____

_____   _____   _____

My child could imitate the following animals today:

_____   _____   _____

_____   _____   _____

#3

My child guessed the following animals today:

_____   _____   _____

_____   _____   _____

My child could make sounds for the following animals today:

_____   _____   _____

_____   _____   _____

My child could imitate the following animals today:

_____   _____   _____

_____   _____   _____

The Five Senses—Sight: "Picture This"

Objective

In this activity, your child will gain physical readiness by becoming aware of his or her sense of sight. This activity gets you and your child involved in using a camera to take pictures and then viewing places, people, and events in photographs. This activity fosters visual memory, small motor skills, and abstract and concrete thinking skills.

What To Do

Younger children love to look at the world around them. In fact, the sense of sight is one of the first senses your child uses. The use of picture taking and viewing allows you to actively encourage your child to become a good observer and interpreter of the environment.

Begin this activity by purchasing an inexpensive (perhaps disposable) camera. Talk with your child about using the camera and then decide where the two of you will go to take pictures. Once at the location, talk about what he or she sees and why it would make a nice picture. Take the film to be developed and review the pictures together. Talk about the differences between pictures and real objects.

What To Say

I bought a little camera at the store. Let's take some photographs. We could take pictures here or maybe go somewhere interesting. We could go to the zoo or the beach. Where would you like to go to take some pictures?

Variations

Let your child begin his or her own photo album with the developed pictures, adding to the collection over time. Review the pictures each time more are added and talk about them.

72

The Five Senses— Sight: "Picture This" (cont.)

Milestone Checklist

☐ My child and I bought our first camera
on_____/_____/_____.

☐ My child and I had our first picture taking experience
on_____/_____/_____.

☐ My child knew how to operate a simple camera
on_____/_____/_____.

☐ My child experienced having pictures developed
on_____/_____/_____.

☐ My child is becoming increasingly aware of things he or she can see.

☐ My child knows the names of the things he or she has photographed.

☐ My child could explain how to take a picture.

Impressions of our first picture taking experience:

_____

_____

Impressions of our first experience getting pictures developed and the results:

_____

_____

My child's favorite pictures are

_____

_____

Activity Repetitions

#2

Impressions of our first experience getting pictures developed and the results:

_____

_____

My child's favorite pictures are

_____

_____

#3

Impressions of our first experience getting pictures developed and the results:

_____

_____

My child's favorite pictures are

_____

_____

The Five Senses—Hearing: "What Can I Hear?"

Objective

In this activity, your child will gain physical readiness by becoming aware of the sense of hearing. Your child will listen and record sounds both indoors and out. This activity fosters auditory memory and concrete thinking.

What To Do

Sounds are all around! As adults, we try to shut out noise, to avoid distractions as we work. But children are fascinated with sound. In this activity, you and your child will listen for interesting sounds, record them, and then play them back.

Begin this activity by getting a new tape for your tape recorder that you could designate just for this purpose. Then you could keep this tape for your child to listen and add to again and again. If you don't have a tape recorder, you could listen to sounds without recording. Whatever works best for you and your child is fine.

Talk with your child about interesting sounds. Ask him or her to name the sounds heard as you are talking. Write the sounds down on a piece of paper and read the words together, if you like. Listen inside your house and then step outside and listen again. Talk together about how the sounds change from inside to outside. The following are some interesting sounds to listen for:

Inside	Outside
bells	birds
clocks ticking	dogs
refrigerator	cats
voices	neighbors
music	lawn mower
television	kids playing
radio	cars
water running	trucks
water dripping	machinery
laughter	crickets
snoring	insects
rain	horns
thunder	sirens
washer	footsteps
	wind

What To Say

Let's listen to all the different sounds we can hear in the house. I hear the washing machine. What do you hear? I hear your brother laughing. I like his laugh. Now, let's go out in the backyard and listen again. I hear the neighbors. Do you hear that tweeting? What is that?

Variations

Use the outdoor sounds for a relaxation tape, recording bird songs or ocean waves, for example.

The Five Senses—Hearing: "What Can I Hear?" *(cont.)*

Milestone Checklist

- ❑ My child made his or her first inside recording on_____/_____/_____.
- ❑ My child made his or her first outside recording on_____/_____/_____.
- ❑ My child could identify the sounds he or she hears in the house on_____/_____/_____.
- ❑ My child could identify the sounds he or she heard outside on_____/_____/_____.
- ❑ My child knew how to operate the tape recorder on_____/_____/_____.
- ❑ My child identified again the sounds he or she recorded on_____/_____/_____.

Observations of My Child's First Recording:

_____

_____

Sounds recorded inside:

_____ _____ _____

Sounds recorded outside:

_____ _____ _____

Activity Repetitions

Observations of My Child's Second Recording:

_____

_____

Sounds recorded inside:

_____ _____ _____

Sounds recorded outside:

_____ _____ _____

Observations of My Child's Third Recording:

_____

_____

Sounds recorded inside:

_____ _____ _____

Sounds recorded outside:

_____ _____ _____

The Five Senses—Smell: "Smells in the Garden"

Objective

In this activity, your child will gain physical readiness by becoming aware of the sense of smell. This activity takes your child to your garden to smell all the different outdoor smells. This activity fosters sense memory as well as abstract and concrete thinking skills.

What To Do

The sense of smell is often not as highly developed in people as many of the other senses. For this activity, you and your child will explore the smells in a garden and outside in general. If you live in a city far from a garden, take to the streets and smell restaurants, bakeries, soap shops, department stores, and other fragrant places. Any place you and your child would like to go "smell hunting" is appropriate.

Begin by talking with your child about smells. Ask him or her what smells there are inside the house. Then ask what you might discover outside. Talk about all the things that are possible and then go outside and find out how many of the things he or she guessed are correct.

Talk about all the different places that you can go "smell hunting." Together, pick a place and go. Compare the smells between one place and another. Some interesting places for smells include the following:

- gas station
- bakery
- nursery
- forest
- beach
- city street
- desert

What To Say

I have been thinking about all the interesting smells we can smell. What do you smell now, in the house? I can smell dinner, and I can smell the fresh laundry. What do you smell? What do you think we might smell outside? Let's go outside and see.

Variations

Make any errand around town an exploration of smell. It is amazing how waiting in line can become fun when you and your child are concentrating on something interesting.

The Five Senses—Smell: "Smells in the Garden" *(cont.)*

Milestone Checklist

☐ My child identified smells in the house
on_____/_____/_____.

☐ My child identified smells outside
on_____/_____/_____.

☐ My child knew the words for a variety of smells.

☐ My child identified smells that are new.

☐ My child could describe smells verbally.

☐ My child could remember and describe smells.

Our First "Smell Hunting" Exploration Was To

_____

General observations of my child:

_____

_____

Smells my child identified today:

_____

_____

New smells:

_____

_____

Activity Repetitions

#2

Our second "smell hunting" exploration was to

_____

General observations of my child:

_____

_____

Smells my child identified today:

_____

_____

New smells:

_____

_____

#3

Our third "smell hunting" exploration was to

_____

General observations of my child:

_____

_____

Smells my child identified today:

_____

_____

New smells:

_____

_____

The Five Senses—Taste: "Diverse Foods"

Objective

In this activity, your child will gain physical readiness by becoming aware of the sense of taste. This activity will encourage your child to experience tastes which will later make new foods at school or other places easier to cope with. This activity fosters sense memory, thinking skills, and curiosity.

What To Do

Experts agree that forcing children to try new foods during the preschool years could cause resistance to those very foods you would love them to eat. However, by using foods your child already loves, you could encourage thinking about the taste and differentiate among several tastes in a nonthreatening, entertaining way. Eventually, this relaxed and nonjudgmental attitude will encourage food exploration at an individual rate.

Begin by gathering three of your child's favorite foods. Talk with him or her about how they taste and why they taste good. Then, put a blindfold on your child and provide him or her a small taste of each. After each taste, pause while you ask which favorite it was. Listen for insight into your child's personal tastes.

What To Say

Let's play a guessing game with your favorite foods. I have three of your favorite foods here. What is this? Yes, it's macaroni and cheese! And this? Yes, it is an apple slice. And this last one? Yes, it is a bowl of cereal. Now, which is your very favorite? Why? Now, let's cover your eyes and let you taste them. Do you know what they are with your eyes closed? Good. Now, let's make a list of all your favorite foods, so we will have it in case we ever forget all the foods you like!

Variations

Use the food list you compile with your child to make your own shopping list. You may be pleasantly surprised to discover the number of foods enjoyed by both you and your child.

The Five Senses—Taste: "Diverse Foods" (cont.)

Milestone Checklist

❑ My child recognized his or her favorite foods by sight.

❑ My child recognized his or her favorite foods by taste.

❑ My child listed his or her favorite foods
on_____/_____/_____.

❑ My child could describe why he or she likes a favorite food.

❑ We played the food guessing game today using these three foods:

_____

_____

My observations about my child's ability to discriminate among tastes are

_____

_____

My child's list of favorite foods includes:

_____ _____ _____

_____ _____ _____

Activity Repetitions

#2

❑ We played the food guessing game today using these three foods:

_____

_____

My observations about my child's ability to discriminate among tastes are

_____

_____

#3

❑ We played the food guessing game today, using these three foods:

_____

_____

My observations about my child's ability to discriminate among tastes are

_____

_____

The Five Senses—Touch: "Touch Collection"

Objective

In this activity, your child will gain physical readiness by becoming more aware of the sense of touch. In this activity, you and your child will make a "Touching Collection" of items that are interesting to touch. This activity fosters sense memory, small motor skills, and concrete and abstract thinking skills.

What To Do

The sense of touch is important to us all. While it isn't one of our main ways of gathering information, the information from touching objects gives our brains useful information. In this activity, your child will have the opportunity to touch things around the house and from nature, and to create a collection of favorites.

Begin this activity by talking with your child about the way things feel. Gather together five objects from inside the house and talk with your child about how they feel when touched. Are they hard? Soft? Does the object feel good to touch or not so good? Why?

Then have your child look at his or her own belongings. Let him or her gather five interesting things to touch by searching for the softest thing in the house or something wet or cold. Go outside and try touching outside objects, repeating a similar process.

What To Say

There are so many great things to touch in our house. I like petting our kitty. She is so soft. Try petting her. What else is soft in our house? Let's look around and see what we can find. Now, let's see what is cold. I know—ice! Let's feel some ice. The floor is cold, too. Let's take our shoes off and feel it with our toes. Now let's find warm things. Your hands are warm. They feel good to hold. Let's find some more.

Variations

Put small items in a shoebox or paper bag and reach in without looking to feel the items. See if your child can guess what the items are without looking. Then look and see!

The Five Senses—Touch: "Touch Collection" *(cont.)*

Milestone Checklist

☐ My child determined when an object is hot
on_____/_____/_____.

☐ My child determined when an object is cold
on_____/_____/_____.

☐ My child determined when an object is hard
on_____/_____/_____.

☐ My child determined when an object is soft
on_____/_____/_____.

☐ My child described how an object felt
on_____/_____/_____.

☐ My child and I collected the following items for our "Touch Collection":

_____   _____   _____

_____   _____   _____

Observations about my child's experience:

_____

_____

_____

_____

_____

Activity Repetitions

#2

_____/_____/_____.

Today we are focusing on_____items.

My child touched these items:

_____   _____   _____

_____   _____   _____

His or her reactions were

_____

_____

#3

_____/_____/_____.

Today we are focusing on_____items.

My child touched these items:

_____   _____   _____

_____   _____   _____

His or her reactions were

_____

_____

At–Home Obstacle Course

Objective

In this activity, your child will gain physical readiness by successfully completing an obstacle course. This activity will increase your child's ability to listen to and carry out directions. This activity fosters coordination, large motor skills, and concrete thinking skills.

What To Do

It's simple to create an at–home obstacle course without adding a thing to your existing environment. By following the course your child will become familiar with the concepts related to the words "around," "over," "under," and "through." Just pick an area inside your house that will work for you and remove all precious and breakable objects. The following are some typical household objects that make it easy for your child to experience the meanings of these words:

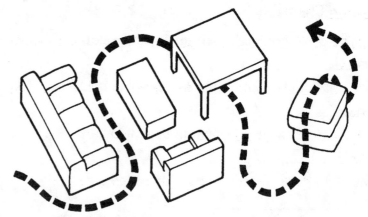

Just set up the obstacle course and lead your child through it. Call it a "walking" obstacle course if you are concerned about your child moving quickly through the house.

Around
- chairs
- tables
- sofa

Over
- stacked books
- pillows
- teddy bear

Under
- table legs
- blanket
- string

Through
- table legs
- doorway
- hallway

What To Say

I have made an obstacle course for us. Let me show you how it works. First, I go around this chair and then I jump over this book. Then I go through the doorway and under this blanket. Next I go around this table and over these three pillows. Finally, I go under this string I have tied here to get to the end. Let's try it!

Variations

If you prefer, create an outdoor course. Patio furniture and children's play equipment will work well.

Go to a public park or playground and create your own obstacle course there. If available, use fitness trail equipment and change the specific tasks to be kid-friendly.

82

At–Home Obstacle Course (cont.)

Milestone Checklist

- ❏ My child understood and demonstrated the meaning of "under."
- ❏ My child understood and demonstrated the meaning of "over."
- ❏ My child understood and demonstrated the meaning of "through."
- ❏ My child understood and demonstrated the meaning of "around."
- ❏ My child finished the obstacle course successfully.

The following is a simple sketch of our first obstacle course:

My child completed the obstacle course on_____/_____/_____.

Observations:

Activity Repetitions

#2

My child completed the obstacle course on_____/_____/_____.

Observations:

_____

_____

_____

_____

#3

My child completed the obstacle course on_____/_____/_____.

Observations:

_____

_____

_____

_____

_____

Buttons, Snaps, and Bows Dressing Contest

Objective

In this activity your child will gain physical readiness by taking part in a "dressing contest" you devise. This activity fosters increased large and small motor skills and coordination, as well as cognitive and concrete thinking skills.

What To Do

It's very important that your child can dress and undress himself or herself before entering school. This kind of mastery ensures that he or she will be able to use the restroom and put on and take off winter clothes. You could make proficient dressing into an interesting contest. All you need is a kitchen timer.

Begin this activity in the morning before your child or you are dressed. First, help your child select what he or she will wear. Choose clothes that are possible to put on completely without assistance. (No back buttons, ties, or zippers.) Then challenge your child to a "dressing contest." The first person to arrive fully dressed at a designated spot in the house wins! (Dress slowly to give your child a chance to win.)

Another idea is to allow your child to set the kitchen timer and play "beat the clock." This is an excellent way to reinforce the same skills without your active participation. Do this activity often to encourage your child's dressing mastery.

What To Say

Let's have a contest to see who can get dressed the fastest. The first person to put on all his or her clothes and sit down at the breakfast table wins. Let's decide together what clothes you would like to wear, and then we can begin. Let's choose things you know you can put on quickly. Is this T-shirt a good choice? How about these jeans? Now let's choose socks and shoes. Great. Now, when I yell "go" from my room, we will both start. Good luck!

Variations

Get the whole family involved in a dressing contest. It will definitely help you get to school on time!

Practice undressing by having "pajama races." Give a small prize to the winner.

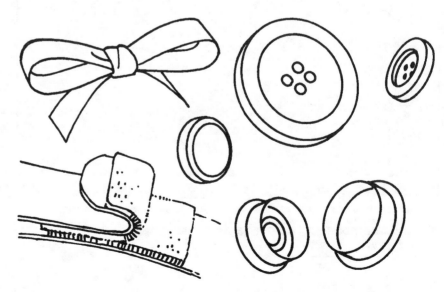

Buttons, Snaps, and Bows Dressing Contest *(cont.)*

My child could put on the following items of clothes with ease:

- ❑ underwear
- ❑ T-shirt
- ❑ sweater
- ❑ shorts
- ❑ bathing suit
- ❑ slacks or jeans
- ❑ sweats
- ❑ gloves
- ❑ socks
- ❑ shoes
- ❑ hat
- ❑ jacket
- ❑ coat
- ❑ boots

Our First "Dressing Contest" Was on_____/_____/____.

I noticed this about my child's ability to dress:

_____

_____

Activity Repetitions

#2

Our Second "Dressing Contest" Was on_____/_____/____.

I noticed this about my child's ability to dress:

_____

_____

_____

_____

_____

#3

Our Third "Dressing Contest" Was on_____/_____/____.

I noticed this about my child's ability to dress:

_____

_____

_____

_____

_____

ABC Yarn Flash Cards

Objective

In this activity your child gains physical readiness by using "ABC Yarn Flash Cards" that you make together. By creating and using these cards, your child will increase small motor skills as well as the ability to understand concrete concepts and comprehend letter symbols. This activity also fosters cognitive thinking skills.

What To Do

Small motor skills are very important in school. Children can't wait to hold crayons or pencils, use scissors, and work with glue. But, if a child is unable to successfully work with these materials, the experience could be very frustrating. The following are simple directions for "ABC Yarn Flash Cards" your child could help make and enjoy using.

Materials

- colored yarn
- glue
- large index cards
- crayons
- scissors

Directions

- Draw the uppercase letters of the alphabet on cards with a crayon.
- Cover the outline of the crayon letter with glue.
- Apply colored yarn to the glue.
- Dry.
- Use the cards like flash cards. Have your child trace the outline of each letter and say the name.

What To Say

Let's make something really neat today. These are called "ABC Yarn Flash Cards." Would you like to help me draw and glue? This is what we do: First, we draw a letter—this is the letter "A." Now, let's cover this letter with glue only on the crayon lines. Next we'll cut a piece of yarn. What color would you like? Now, let's press it on the glue. When it dries, we can trace the letter with our fingers. There!

Variations

Create "Number Flash Cards" in the same way, or write your child's name and make a yarn name plate.

ABC Yarn Flash Cards (cont.)

Milestone Checklist

❑ My child used scissors on_____/_____/_____.

❑ My child manipulated glue on_____/_____/_____.

❑ My child drew with a crayon on_____/_____/_____.

❑ My child traced a letter with his or her finger and said its name on_____/_____/_____.

❑ My child copied a letter from an example on_____/_____/_____.

❑ My child wrote a letter from memory on_____/_____/_____.

Observations about making "ABC Yarn Cards" with my child:

_____

_____

_____

_____

_____

_____

_____

Activity Repetitions

#2

Letters my child could identify:

_____ _____ _____

_____ _____ _____

Letters my child could copy:

_____ _____ _____

_____ _____ _____

Letters my child could write from memory:

_____ _____ _____

_____ _____ _____

#3

Letters my child could identify:

_____ _____ _____

_____ _____ _____

Letters my child could copy:

_____ _____ _____

_____ _____ _____

Letters my child could write from memory:

_____ _____ _____

_____ _____ _____

"Simon Says" Body Parts

Objective

In this activity, your child will gain physical readiness by learning to identify the parts of his or her body by name. This activity helps your child make the connection between words and their meanings as well as increasing the concrete thinking skills necessary to respond physically to oral requests. Large motor skills will also be developed.

What To Do

Simon says, "Touch your foot!" Simon says, "Touch your ear!" This wonderful old children's game has been played by nearly everyone. By simply directing your child to identify specific parts of his or her body, you could modify the game to teach your child the names for body parts or determine what parts are already known or need to be learned.

Begin this activity, if necessary, by teaching your child how to play "Simon Says!" Once your child is comfortable with the game, try it by naming body parts or asking him or her to identify them.

Look at the checklist on the following page for a basic list of names for parts of the body that your child should know before entering school. Then, have fun!

What To Say

Let's play a game called "Simon Says!" First, I'll be "Simon." When I ask you to do something, I will say it like this: Simon says, "Touch your toe!" Could you do that? Great job! Now, I will try some more. Are you ready? Listen carefully.

Variations

Let your child be "Simon." Ask your child to name the parts of your body that he or she wants you to identify. This will make it necessary for your child to name the parts of the body orally, rather than respond to your requests.

Play a more physical version of "Simon Says" outside. Ask your child to run, skip, jump, hop, or anything else that requires physical movement. Notice basic large motor skills and coordination.

"Simon Says" Body Parts (cont.)

Milestone Checklist

My child could identify the following body parts:

- ❑ head
- ❑ shoulders
- ❑ neck
- ❑ chest
- ❑ tummy
- ❑ arms
- ❑ hands
- ❑ fingers
- ❑ thumb
- ❑ legs
- ❑ feet
- ❑ toes
- ❑ hair
- ❑ eyes
- ❑ skin
- ❑ mouth
- ❑ ears
- ❑ eyebrow
- ❑ chin

My child played "Simon Says" Body Parts for the first time on _____/_____/_____.

I noticed this about his or her ability to respond to directions:

_____

_____

Activity Repetitions

#2

My child played "Simon Says" Body Parts for the second time on_____/_____/_____.

I noticed this about his or her ability to respond to directions:

_____

_____

#3

My child played "Simon Says" Body Parts for the third time on _____/_____/_____.

I noticed this about his or her ability to respond to directions:

_____

_____

Emotional Readiness Overview

What Is Emotional Readiness?

Emotional readiness is your child's appropriate level of emotional maturity based on his or her own individual development. There is a wide range of what is appropriate emotionally at any time, not just for children but for people of any age. Just as some people weep at movies while others cry rarely or never, some children will cry more frequently than others. Children feel all the different emotions that adults do, but they haven't yet learned to control them. This makes children more authentic with their feelings but could also make communication with them difficult at times.

Everyone Has Feelings

In the course of any given day we might feel angry, loving, silly, frustrated, annoyed, compassionate, humorous, afraid, or shy. These are all normal emotions and children certainly feel them, too. To be emotionally ready for school implies that a child has the ability to deal with emotions in a way that doesn't detract too often from the rest of the group and is on the same general level with his or her peers.

Different Children, Different Temperaments

Remember, your child has his or her own unique temperament or pattern of emotional responses. The key to helping your child become emotionally ready for school is to help him or her learn to practice many ways of handling feelings. It is as important to name and validate the feelings of your child as it is to teach him or her to deal appropriately with feelings in group situations. The activities that follow in this section will help you do just that. Use the checklist on the following page to determine your child's current level of emotional readiness.

Emotional Readiness Checklist

❑ Seems to function well without parent for several hours at a time

❑ Feels comfortable most of the time about parent's leaving; may react emotionally with tears or fear, but can be distracted fairly easily and resumes activity

❑ Is able to communicate well enough to tell an adult if he or she is sick, or in trouble, or needs assistance

❑ Has had a variety of opportunities to interact with children and adults and has done so for the most part with enjoyment

❑ Seems fairly comfortable trying new things or being in new situations

❑ Has the ability to be quiet for short periods of time

❑ Understands the meanings of feeling words and knows how to explain when he or she is sad, angry, scared, or happy

❑ Doesn't respond with violence in situations of anger; displays self-control by not hitting, biting, kicking, or otherwise engaging in physical behavior

❑ Is able to rest comfortably at rest time, and seems relaxed after a nap or quiet time

❑ Isn't offended by basic rules or requests from an adult in authority

❑ Has developed a long enough attention span to understand and react appropriately to a short sequence of directions

❑ Can tolerate disappointment and frustration reasonably well

❑ Is beginning to learn empathic behavior toward others, i.e., understands when someone else is angry, sad, happy, or afraid

❑ After crying or being angry, resumes regular activity within a reasonable length of time

When I Feel . . .

I feel sad sometimes.

When I feel sad, I might cry.

My mother says it's all right to feel sad and it's all right to cry.

But she also told me some ways to make myself feel better.

92   *© Teacher Created Materials, Inc.*

When I Feel . . . (cont.)

When I feel sad, I can try these things.

I can think of something happy.

I can do something to make myself feel happy.

I can do something to make someone else feel happy.

When I Feel . . . (cont.)

I feel angry sometimes.

When I feel angry, I want to yell and scream and throw things!

My mother says it's all right to feel angry as long as I don't hurt anyone.

But she also told me some ways to make myself feel better.

When I Feel . . . (cont.)

When I feel angry, I can try these things.

I can go into my room and yell and scream.

I can get a piilow and punch it.

I can go outside and run or ride my bicycle.

When I Feel . . . (cont.)

I feel scared sometimes.

When I feel scared, sometimes I try to act brave, but other times I just act scared.

My mother says it's all right to feel scared.

But she also told me some ways to make myself feel better.

When I Feel . . . *(cont.)*

When I feel scared, I can try these things.

I can stay away from what I'm afraid of.

I can face what I'm afraid of and find out more about it.

I can talk to somebody about how I feel.

When I Feel . . . *(cont.)*

I feel lonely sometimes.

When I feel lonely, I want someone to play with.

My mother says it's all right to feel lonely and it's all right to be alone.

But she also told me some ways to make myself feel better.

98

When I Feel . . . *(cont.)*

When I feel lonely, I can try these things.

I can call a friend on the telephone.

I can ask my mother to invite someone over to play.

I can do something that is fun to do by myself, like draw or look at books.

When I Feel . . . (cont.)

I feel very peaceful sometimes.

When I feel peaceful, I like to think and dream.

My mother says it's wonderful to feel peaceful.

She asked me to tell her some of the things I think and dream about.

When I Feel . . . *(cont.)*

When I feel peaceful, these are some of the things I think and dream about.

I think about the rain and all the wonderful stories I've been told.

I think about all the people I love.

I dream of all the great adventures I'll have when I am older.

When I Feel . . . (cont.)

I feel very happy sometimes.

When I feel happy, I smile and laugh.

My mother says it makes her happy to see me happy.

She asked me to tell her some of the things that make me feel that way.

When I Feel . . . (cont.)

When I feel happy, these are some of the things that make me feel that way.

My favorite toys make me feel happy and so do my favorite foods.

Smiling faces and big hugs make me feel happy.

But sometimes I just feel happy for no reason at all!

School Tour

Objective

In this activity, your child will increase his or her emotional readiness for school by gaining some familiarity with future surroundings. Taking several trips to your child's future school will increase feelings of mastery, self-esteem and empowerment, safety, security, and confidence.

What To Do

Begin this activity as soon as you know which school your child will be attending. (In fact, this activity could be done each time your child will be going to any new setting with regularity.) Talk with your child about the new school and say that you are going to make a visit together. Plan a few casual visits to the location, perhaps even before going with your child to officially meet the teacher or see the facility.

For example, start by driving by the school and saying that this will be the school he or she will go to someday. Every time you pass the school, mention this fact and talk about all the wonderful things about school. If permissible, pack a picnic and take it to the school grounds to eat it on the weekend. If possible, peek in the windows and let your child see what a classroom looks like and the kinds of art and other work that are displayed. Let your child play in the playground. If the school your child is attending is within walking distance, walk there with your child on a regular basis so he or she can begin to see where it is in relation to your house.

What To Say

Pretty soon, when you are five, you are going to go to kindergarten. Let's drive by and take a look at your school. We could go on the playground and try the swings and slide and take a look at it.

Let's take a look around. We might look in the windows and see what the classrooms look like. Another day, I will bring you when the children are in school so you can see what a fun place it is going to be.

Variations

Talk to the administrators at the school your child will be attending and find out when you might visit with your child. Attend school programs that are open to the public with your child, such as plays, holiday programs, and craft fairs. This will give your child a chance to see what goes on at the school he or she will be attending and see the children involved in activities.

School Tour (cont.)

Milestone Checklist

❑ My child had a basic understanding about beginning school on _____/_____/_____.

❑ My child has visited his or her future school_____/_____/_____.

❑ My child returned to visit his or her future school on_____/_____/_____.

❑ My child met his or her teacher on_____/_____/_____.

❑ My child seems generally positive about attending school.

❑ My child has a general understanding about what happens at school.

❑ My child will attend school beginning on_____/_____/_____.

My child's initial impressions about going to school are

_____

_____

We have discussed the following things about going to school:

_____

_____

After our first visit my child felt

_____

_____

Activity Repetitions

#2

On my child's second visit to school, we did the following:

_____

_____

My child voiced these opinions and/or concerns:

_____

_____

I assisted him or her with any concerns by

_____

_____

#3

On my child's third visit to school, we did the following:

_____

_____

My child voiced these opinions and/or concerns:

_____

_____

I assisted him or her with any concerns by

_____

_____

Phone Number Song and Calling Home Game

Objective

In this activity, your child will learn his or her phone number and also how to dial it from a public phone. This activity increases your child's confidence, sense of autonomy, mastery, and self-esteem. This activity fosters your child's sense of competence and knowledge and understanding of appropriate responses in difficult or emergency situations.

What To Do

It's never too early to teach your child his or her phone number. In case you become separated, or if she or he is in a situation where you are needed, being able to identify his or her phone number is important. Begin this activity, by talking about it. Let him or her see you dial the phone. Tell him or her your phone number. Say the numbers when you dial from a pay phone. Practice the numbers from one to ten with him or her, and show him or her the symbols for the numbers.

Then pick any children's song with which your child is very familiar with and sing your phone number to that song. Here is an example using "Row, Row, Row Your Boat":

Six...one...nine...five...five,

five, one, two, four, three,

This is the number to call at home,

It's as easy as can be!

Or just make up a song that works with your number without concern about rhyming—the point is to attach a tune to the memorization of numbers. You will find your child thinks this is fun.

Then, when you are at pay phones, let your child call home, either to talk to someone or leave a message on the answering machine. Make this a ritual when going out to do errands and in no time your child will know how to use a phone.

What To Say

I have a new song to teach you to help you learn our phone number. Let's sing it. After you learn our phone number, I will let you use a pay phone to call home all by yourself. This way if you ever need to call home, you will know how!

Variations

Give your child a few quarters to keep in his or her school bag for phone calls after starting school or buy a low-cost phone card for emergencies.

Phone Number Song and Calling Home Game (cont.)

Milestone Checklist

☐ My child knows and can say his or her first and last name
on_____/_____/_____.

☐ My child knows and could say my first and last name
on_____/_____/_____.

☐ My child could repeat his or her phone number when asked
on_____/_____/_____.

☐ My child could sing our own phone number song
on_____/_____/_____.

☐ My child could identify a public telephone
on_____/_____/_____.

☐ My child could dial our telephone on_____/_____/_____.

I have created a simple phone song to the tune of this children's song:

_____

_____

The words to the song are

_____

_____

My child has voiced these ideas, opinions, or concerns about using a phone:

_____

_____

I responded to my child's concerns by

_____

_____

Activity Repetitions

#2

The following are my impressions about my child's familiarity with the phone:

_____

_____

My child's comfort level with using a phone is_____.

We need to work on the following:

_____

_____

#3

The following are my impressions about my child's familiarity with the phone:

_____

_____

My child's comfort level with using a phone is_____.

We need to work on the following:

_____

_____

"People Who Could Help" Game

Objective

In this activity, your child will learn to identify helpful adults. This activity will increase his or her emotional readiness for school by increasing confidence and security and by developing the ability to make decisions based on good information.

What To Do

Begin this activity by talking with your child about people who can help. Look for books in your public library or articles in your home encyclopedia about police and firefighters, doctors and nurses, etc. Visit a hospital or your own pediatrician and let your child see what doctors and nurses look like and explain how they help. Call your local police station or fire station and ask if you could drop by to let your child meet a police officer or fire fighter. Many stations will be more than happy to help you regarding this.

Watch for community events in which helpful people are present. Attend with your child the parades, fairs, or other events sponsored by these departments or call and find out what kinds of programs they have available for children.

The main idea is to talk with your child about what to do if he or she needs help. Explain that he or she could go to these people and ask for help or to use the phone. Reinforce these concepts by talking about them often.

What To Say

If you ever need help, there are people called police officers who could help you. Let's find a book at the library that has pictures of a police station, and then one day we will go meet a police officer. Police help people who are lost or who need help. If you need help and I am not here, you could ask a police officer or a firefighter. (Discuss other people your child knows who are appropriate people to go to for help.)

Variations

Talk with your child about calling 911. You will need to determine if your child is old enough to understand the difference between playing with the phone and calling 911 for "fun" and making a serious call for help. It's common for many young children not to be able to differentiate between a real need and just making the call because they know how.

"People Who Could Help" Game *(cont.)*

Milestone Checklist

☐ My child could identify a picture of a police officer
on_____/_____/_____.

☐ My child could identify a picture of a doctor
on_____/_____/_____.

☐ My child could identify a picture of a nurse
on_____/_____/_____.

☐ My child could identify a picture of a fire fighter
on_____/_____/_____.

☐ My child identified these helping professionals in real life
on_____/_____/_____.

☐ My child met his or her doctor on_____/_____/_____.

☐ My child met a police officer or firefighter
on_____/_____/_____.

I decided to introduce my child to people who could help by

_____

_____

_____

Our first experience had these results:

_____

_____

_____

Activity Repetitions

#2

For our second experience in becoming familiar with people who could help, we did the following:

_____

_____

Our second experience had these results:

_____

_____

_____

#3

For our third experience in becoming familiar with people who could help, we did the following:

_____

_____

Our third experience had these results:

_____

_____

_____

"Love You" Photo Album

Objective

In this activity, your child will increase his or her emotional readiness by increasing his or her overall sense of security, happiness, love, and comfort. By creating a "Love You" photo album, your child will have a constant, portable reminder of those who love him or her.

What To Do

Everyone likes to have some kind of token or remembrance of people he or she loves. Sometimes parents forget that children feel all of the same feelings and longings that they do with one important exception—they lack the emotional maturity to understand and cope with their feelings on the same level that adults do.

Preparing for your child some tangible reminders of the people he or she loves and letting your child be part of the process is an excellent way to reinforce feelings of love and acceptance.

Get a child's wallet or a small photo album and let your child fill it with pictures of important people. Let your child choose the pictures he or she wants and talk about those people. Remember to include people not seen on a daily basis, like grandparents or cousins, or even pictures of important pets. As you put together this little photo album, reinforce the idea that the people included in it return or share your child's affection.

What To Say

I was thinking that you might like to have pictures of the people you love in a wallet just as I do. Look at my wallet with me. Here is a picture of you, here is one of Dad and here are Grammy and our cat. When I am by myself sometimes, I look at these pictures and they make me happy because I think about how much I love you and how much you love me.

Let's pick some pictures for you that we can put in your own wallet. Here is a picture of me. And I love you the most! Now, what other pictures would you like? (Discuss this with your child.)

Variations

Consider a bulletin board for your child's room for important pictures. Or designate a spot in your house as a "love board" for pictures. Or go to a photo booth with your child and for a few dollars you could have fun making pictures that could be replaced again and again inexpensively.

110

"Love You" Photo Album (cont.)

Milestone Checklist

☐ My child could identify his or her family members in photographs on_____/_____/_____.

☐ My child could identify the people he or she loves on_____/_____/_____.

☐ My child chose pictures for his or her own "Love You" photo album on_____/_____/_____.

☐ My child created his or her own "Love You" photo album on_____/_____/_____.

When I explained about making the "Love You" photo album my child reacted by _____.

We discussed the following:

_____

_____

My child chose the following people's pictures:

_____

_____

My general observations are

_____

_____

Activity Repetitions

#2

I have noticed my child using the photo album this way:

_____

_____

My child changed or added pictures to his or her album on_____/_____/_____.

General observations:

_____

_____

#3

I have noticed my child using the photo album this way:

_____

_____

My child changed or added pictures to his or her album on_____/_____/_____.

General observations:

_____

_____

"What If . . . ?" Game

Objective

In this activity, your child will become emotionally ready for school by thinking through possible situations and deciding what may be best to do in each one. This activity will increase confidence and provide a sense of empowerment, mastery, and self-esteem, as well as provide practice thinking about concrete situations and cause and effect relationships.

What To Do

Like many of the activities that will increase your child's emotional readiness, this one requires that you talk with and listen to your child. Therefore, nothing is needed for this activity except your interest and attention to your child in conversation.

The purpose of this activity is to go over possible situations with your child and talk about appropriate responses. Before beginning, think about the situations you would like to prepare your child for and the response you would like him or her to have in each one.

Start out by saying "What if . . . ?" and then fill in the blank with a simple situation. Then listen to his or her response. After hearing his or her response, provide any additional information about the best way to handle the situation. Do this occasionally on different subjects until your child has an understanding of the basic responses that are important. Be careful to watch for signs of stress in your child and make the "what if" sessions short and sweet.

What To Say

I want to talk with you about what we could do if there is ever a fire. What if there were a fire in the neighbor's house and we saw it? What should we do? Calling the fire department is a good idea. How could we do that? We could dial 911. We only dial 911 if it's a real emergency. An emergency is when we need help and we can't help ourselves. What if it's a little tiny fire on our own stove? We might be able to use our fire extinguisher.

Variations

From knowing your own child, you know that there are certain situations that are important to you both that you will want to touch on with this activity. Talk with the other adults in your house about this activity and how you are talking with your child so that you have their support.

"What If . . .?" Game (cont.)

Milestone Checklist

- ❑ My child understood the word "emergency" on_____/_____/_____.
- ❑ My child understood what to do if he or she is lost on_____/_____/_____.
- ❑ My child understood what to do if I don't arrive on time on_____/_____/_____.
- ❑ My child could explain verbally if he or she isn't feeling well on_____/_____/_____.
- ❑ My child understood my rules about strangers on_____/_____/_____.
- ❑ My child knew at least one neighbor on_____/_____/_____.
- ❑ My child could walk to a neighbor's house unassisted on_____/_____/_____.
- ❑ My child understood when to call 911 on_____/_____/_____.

My child and I discussed the following "What if . . .?" situations:

_____

_____

My child and I have role-played the following "What if . . .?" situations:

_____

_____

Observations:

_____

_____

Activity Repetitions

#2

Today my child and I discussed the following "What if . . .?" situations:

_____

_____

Today we role-played the following "What if . . .?" situations:

_____

_____

Observations:

_____

_____

#3

Today my child and I discussed the following "What if . . .?" situations:

_____

_____

Today we role-played the following "What if . . .?" situations:

_____

_____

Observations:

_____

_____

Love Notes

Objective

In this activity, your child will increase emotional readiness for school by writing and receiving love notes from you. This activity will increase self-esteem and worth, empathy, comfort, and security.

What To Do

Children as well as adults need to hear they are loved. Everyone could use the positive reinforcement of being told he or she is loved and cared for, liked and respected. Giving your child a tangible reminder of your love provides something concrete to refer to again and again.

Begin this activity by taking a piece of paper and outlining a heart with a pen, crayon, or felt pen. Be as elaborate or as simple as you wish. An easy idea would be to cut out a number of hearts from construction paper and keep these ready for writing your child love notes.

Write your child a simple love note and read it to him or her. If you do this on a regular basis, you will reinforce the comfort, love, and security of your child as well. (Not to mention the alphabet and word recognition involved in writing and reading notes together!)

What To Say

I made you a special love note on a heart. It is to show you how much I love you. Do you want to look at it? Here, let me read it to you. Would you like to make me a love note, too? I have cut out some colored hearts for us to write and draw on, and we can use these anytime to write each other love notes.

Variations

Work together to make love notes for other family members. Keep love notes simple. "I love you," or "You are great!" will make your child happy.

Love Notes (cont.)

Milestone Checklist

❑ I created my first love note to my child
on_____/_____/_____.

❑ I read the love note to my child on_____/_____/_____.

❑ My child created a love note for me with my assistance
on_____/_____/_____.

❑ My child created a love note for another family member
on_____/_____/_____.

❑ My child created a love note unassisted
on_____/_____/_____.

❑ My child read a love note unassisted
on_____/_____/_____.

My first love note to my child read:

_____

_____

My second love note to my child read:

_____

_____

My overall observations of our love-note giving experiences is

_____

_____

Activity Repetitions

Memorable love notes:

_____/_____/_____ Contents of note

_____

_____

_____/_____/_____ Contents of note

_____

_____

_____/_____/_____ Contents of note

_____

_____

_____/_____/_____ Contents of note

_____

_____

_____/_____/_____ Contents of note

_____

_____

"How Do I Feel?" Game

Objective

In this activity, your child will increase emotional readiness for school by being better able to understand and recognize feelings and appropriate at-school behavior for feelings. This activity will increase your child's mastery over emotions and his or her sense of self-worth and self-acceptance.

What To Do

Young children are new to the experience of understanding their emotions. By helping them identify how they are feeling, you can give them the building blocks by which they will later become emotionally mature people and make appropriate and self-knowledgeable choices about their emotions and how they choose to handle these emotions.

Begin this activity by getting into the practice of sharing how you feel with your child. Keep your explanations simple and to the point. Share good feelings (happiness, joy, peace, excitement) as well as those that aren't so happy (sadness, anger, annoyance, frustration). Remember, any negative emotions you might feel may make your child feel he or she is doing something wrong or is unloved. Make the distinction very clear between your feelings and your child's feelings from the beginning. Make it again and again and again because preschoolers often don't understand things the first or sometimes even the hundredth time.

When you sense that your child is experiencing an emotion, say "What kind of feelings are you having right now?" If your child is unsure, make a couple of suggestions. You might ask about feeling happy because of playing with a sibling or feeling excited because a holiday is coming.

What To Say

I notice you seem to be having some feelings about the show you are watching. How does it make you feel? Yes, I think it is sad when the dog is lost, too. How will you feel if the little boy finds him? Yes, I will too. Do you ever watch shows that make you feel scared? Which ones?

Variations

Share how you feel when your emotions are strong and tell your child why. Ask his or her opinion on the same subject and listen nonjudgmentally.

"How Do I Feel?" Game (cont.)

Milestone Checklist

☐ My child could identify when he or she felt happy
on_____/_____/_____.

☐ My child could identify when he or she felt angry
on_____/_____/_____.

☐ My child could identify when he or she felt sad
on_____/_____/_____.

☐ My child could identify when he or she felt frustrated
on_____/_____/_____.

☐ My child could identify when he or she felt tired
on_____/_____/_____.

☐ My child could communicate when he or she felt happy
on_____/_____/_____.

☐ My child could communicate when he or she felt angry
on_____/_____/_____.

☐ My child could communicate when he or she felt sad
on_____/_____/_____.

☐ My child could communicate when he or she felt
frustrated on_____/_____/_____.

☐ My child could communicate when he or she felt tired
on_____/_____/_____.

Today I discussed the following emotions with my child:

_____

General impressions about my child's ability to understand
these emotions:

_____

Activity Repetitions

#2

Today I discussed the following emotions with my child:

_____

_____

General observations about my child's beliefs and ideas:

_____

_____

General impressions about my child's ability to understand
these emotions:

_____

_____

#3

Today I discussed the following emotions with my child:

_____

_____

General observations about my child's beliefs and ideas:

_____

_____

General impressions about my child's ability to understand
these emotions:

_____

"What Can I Do to Feel Better?" Game

Objective

In this activity, your child will gain emotional readiness by becoming aware of things to do to reduce his or her own stress and relax. This activity increases self-esteem and confidence and comfort and security.

What To Do

Generally, adults understand when they are stressed. But often adults fail to realize that children, even young children, can become very stressed too. It is important to teach young children ways that they can relax in order to help them self-monitor and control their behavior.

Begin this activity by noticing the ways your child relaxes and encouraging them. Remember, we all need a way to relax and any way that someone relaxes, as long as it is not harmful to anyone, is fine. Many children have a special blanket or a stuffed friend, or they still may suck their thumbs or use a pacifier. If your child has a relaxation behavior for which he or she might be teased at school, like thumb sucking, help find a different way to relax. You might suggest thumb sucking at home but taking a small stuffed bear to school for rest time instead. It's very important to let children find positive ways to cope with stress. Talk with your child about other ways to relax that can be done alone. The following two methods are designed for preschoolers.

Pretty Picture

Have your child think of a happy thought or visualize a fun event or calm setting such as the beach. Tell your child that whenever he or she is feeling upset, a happy thought or picture will make him or her feel better.

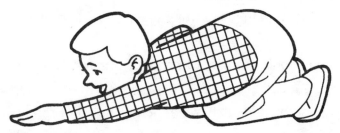

Energy Elevator

Have your child raise a hand in the air. The raised hand is the "energy elevator." As your child brings the hand down to the "bottom floor," the energy comes down too, and relaxation follows. Practice this with your child.

What To Say

Let's try a new game that will help us feel calm and peaceful. I call it "pretty picture." Let's think of something that makes us feel happy and then see it in our minds. When we feel upset, we can always think of this pretty picture, and it will make us feel better.

Variations

Talk with your child's new teacher and find out the policy for taking a blanket or toy that the child loves to school for rest time.

"What Can I Do To Feel Better?" Game (cont.)

Milestone Checklist

❑ My child understood when he or she felt stress on_____/_____/_____.

❑ My child could explain orally when he or she felt stress on_____/_____/_____.

❑ My child could use several methods to relax on_____/_____/_____.

❑ My child responded to my suggestion to use one of these methods on_____/_____/_____.

My child and I discussed what can be done to feel better. My impressions of the conversation were

_____

_____

My child tried the following relaxation method:

_____

_____

My impressions are

_____

_____

Activity Repetitions

#2

My child's stressful situation:

_____

_____

My child's reaction and choices:

_____

_____

#3

My child's stressful situation:

_____

_____

My child's reaction and choices:

_____

_____

Lunchbox ID Plate

Objective

In this activity, your child will gain increased emotional readiness for school by creating a school lunchbox identification plate. This activity will foster an increase in mastery and self-esteem and confidence and security and will provide identification for your child in case of an emergency.

What To Do

It's very important for your child to be able to identify himself or herself by first and last names, phone number, and address. Creating a lunchbox ID plate will help your child become increasingly familiar with all these important facts.

Begin this activity by getting your child a lunch box, wallet, or backpack that will be used daily. The ID card can go in any of these, so choose the one that you believe is most appropriate.

Materials

- small index card
- fine-tip felt pen
- laminating contact paper
- scissors, tape, or glue

With your child write the following information on the card as the example shows.

Example

```
┌─────────────────────────────────────────┐
│         Identification Card              │
│                                          │
│  Name:___Helena Mass_____    │
│                                          │
│  Address: 2709 West Street_____    │
│                                          │
│  Phone: __(602) 398-3332_____    │
└─────────────────────────────────────────┘
```

What To Say

Let's make an identification plate for your new lunchbox (wallet or backpack). That way if it gets lost at school, someone can return it to you. First, we have to get a card. What do you think we should write on it so someone would know it's yours? Your name? Right. And we should write my name, too, and our phone number and address. Let's do that now.

Variations

Use other practical experiences as opportunities for your child to learn your phone number and address. Show him or her the mail addressed to you and encourage relatives to write your child letters or send cards. Ask your child to make the recording for your telephone answering machine. All of these are excellent, practical ways to learn this information.

Lunchbox ID Plate (cont.)

Milestone Checklist

☐ My child knew his or her first and last names
on_____/_____/_____.

☐ My child could say his or her first and last names
on_____/_____/_____.

☐ My child could read his or her first and last names
on_____/_____/_____.

☐ My child could write his or her first and last names
on_____/_____/_____.

☐ On_____/_____/_____my child and I made his or her
lunchbox ID plate.

My impressions of this experience are

_____

_____

My impressions about my child's ability to identify himself or
herself:

_____

_____

Activity Repetitions

#2

My child identified himself or herself in these situations:

_____

_____

My observations:

_____

_____

#3

My child identified himself or herself in these situations:

_____

_____

My observations:

_____

_____

Special Time

Objective

This activity gives your child increased emotional readiness by creating a regular special time between the two of you (or three of you), fostering and nurturing intimacy, communication, and a sense of security for your child.

What To Do

It's easy to forget to make special time with a child in our busy world. It's a challenge to get a child bathed, fed, and dressed every day, much less earn the money needed to keep the child fed, clothed, and housed.

Begin this activity by setting aside a time every day that you and your child can rely on as your own "special time" together. Make this at a convenient, reliable time that will always be a constant, because it is very important to make it something your child can count on.

After you decide what time of each day will be your special time, talk about it with your child. Try not to let anything or anyone stand in the way of having this time with your child. You might read a book together or take a walk at a favorite spot—anything where the two (or three) of you can be together alone with time to talk. This activity can be something you do to increase your level of communication and intimacy as long as your child is at home.

What To Say

Let's make the time before you go to bed every night our very own special time where we are all by ourselves, just us. We don't have to do anything special. It will just give us time that is always ours to talk or read or whatever we want and it will be just for us.

Variations

Try a number of different places and activities with your child to see which ones encourage the best communication between the two (or among the three) of you. You might notice that you always talk about things driving home from school in the car or that you love to sit on the porch together and watch the sunset. Every child and parent is different, and it's important to find the special time together that works best for both of you.

122

Special Time (cont.)

Milestone Checklist

❑ My child and I had a designated "special time" on_____/_____/_____.

❑ My child felt comfortable sharing his or her emotions with me on_____/_____/_____.

❑ My child felt free to ask me for special time.

❑ My child was able to confide in me.

❑ My child and I planned our special time to be

_____

Observations about our first special time:

_____

_____

_____

Other ideas for alternative "special times":

_____

_____

_____

Activity Repetitions

_____/_____/_____

This "special time" was memorable because of the following:

_____

_____

_____

Other observations of this special time:

_____

_____

_____

_____/_____/_____

This "special time" was memorable because of the following:

_____

_____

_____

Other observations of this special time:

_____

_____

_____

"What Do I Need?" Game

Objective

In this activity, your child will gain emotional readiness for school by being able to communicate feelings and needs with language. This activity fosters a respectful assertiveness that will also give your child the ability to say "No" in appropriate situations. This activity increases the ability to understand language, communicate orally, and think about concrete ideas and cause-and-effect relationships.

What To Do

Young children are often at a disadvantage because they do not communicate well with oral language and may not recognize or label their own feelings.

Begin this activity by becoming consciously more aware of both your own and your child's feelings. Gather pictures from old magazines or newspapers or use books that your child has in his or her personal library or even library books — any material that shows people's faces will do.

When you read a story with your child and see a picture of a person, talk about how that person might be feeling. If you are reading a book, and the author talks about how the person is feeling, discuss that feeling. Ask your child what he or she feels that person needs. For example, if it's a picture of a crying child, maybe the child needs a kiss or a bandage from his or her mother. Make this kind of discussion about feelings a part of your everyday conversation.

When noticing that your child is upset, angry, frustrated, or feeling any other emotion, ask him or her to use words to tell you his or her needs. This gives your child an opportunity to think and make a connection between feelings, thoughts, expression, and action.

What To Say

Let's talk about what the little girl in this picture is feeling. She is crying. What does that mean to you? Why do you cry? What do you need when you cry? What do you think this little girl needs?

With your own child, you might say the following: I can tell you are upset. What do you need? Can you tell me in words?

Variations

Practice this behavior with all members of your family. You will find that adults as well as children can learn how to communicate more clearly and that the whole family begins to have greater respect for each other's feelings.

124

"What Do I Need?" Game (cont.)

Milestone Checklist

☐ My child communicated simple information to me
on_____/_____/_____.

☐ My child communicated his or her wishes or desires to me
on_____/_____/_____.

☐ My child communicated anger appropriately in public
on_____/_____/_____.

☐ My child communicated frustration appropriately
on_____/_____/_____.

☐ My child named and discussed things that angered him
or her on_____/_____/_____.

Experience One

I asked my child what he or she needed and the response was

_____

_____

My response to him or her was

_____

_____

The result was

_____

_____

Experience Two

I asked my child what he or she needed and the response was

_____

_____

My response to him or her was

_____

_____

The result was

_____

_____

Experience Three

I asked my child what he or she needed and the response was

_____

_____

My response to him or her was

_____

_____

The result was

_____

_____

Social Readiness Overview

What Is Social Readiness?

Social readiness is your child's appropriate level of social maturity based on his or her own individual development. When your child enters school, he or she must be socialized enough to get along in the school environment. There are some basic social skills, a midpoint, that all children entering school should have. But aside from these basics—using the restroom unassisted, being fully toilet trained, following the simplest directions, and getting along with other children without hurting anyone else or making them unhappy, there is a varying level of social skills in every classroom.

Everyone Relates To Others

Getting along in the world is a skill. We learn to experience empathy, to listen, and to tolerate differences. We learn about the feelings, viewpoints, and opinions of others. We can help our children by teaching the "social graces" that we prize, knowing that good manners and polite behavior are expressions of values such as kindness, thoughtfulness, and sensitivity to others.

Different Children, Different Interpersonal Styles

Everyone is different. Children may be little and unaware, but they still have their own special ways of interacting—a style, a personality, a deeper sense of who they are that affects how they relate to others. We can celebrate and tolerate the different qualities and personalities of others, starting with ourselves and—so importantly—our children.

The activities in the following section explore and encourage acceptable social behavior. Use the checklist on the following page to determine your child's current level of social readiness.

126

Social Readiness Checklist

Psychological Readiness

❑ Feels good about himself or herself and about his or her own achievements in many areas

❑ Recognizes that other children want to feel good, too

❑ Knows what private property is, even if he or she does not always manage to respect the property of others or to insist successfully that others respect his or her property

❑ Understands the concept of sharing (both things and ideas) even though he or she may not choose to share

❑ Understands that there are rules even though he or she may not yet always remember or choose to observe them

Practical Readiness

❑ Has basic table manners and knows their importance in making mealtimes a pleasant experience for himself or herself as well as for others

❑ Knows and uses the words, "please" and "thank you," and understands that their use makes people appreciative

❑ Knows how to use the toilet and has had experience in using public restroom facilities

❑ Has some basic relaxation techniques that make it possible for him or her to remain quiet for short periods, such as a school rest time

❑ Understands the idea of taking turns and is able to put this concept into practice without becoming frustrated or angry

❑ Understands and puts into practice basic safety rules, especially those connected with traffic safety

❑ Has met and feels comfortable talking to some of the people in your neighborhood

❑ Understands and has had experience in helping others

❑ Recognizes and can comment on and discuss the qualities that make other people nice to know

Crabby Carl Goes to School

It seemed as if Carl had always been crabby.

When he was a baby, his mommy spoke so sweetly to him,
  But he just grunted, "Hmpf!"

His daddy said, "How's my little tiger?"

But Carl just turned away.

Crabby Carl Goes to School (cont.)

Even his older sister, Angela, brought him toys to play with and chocolate chip cookies to eat.

Crabby Carl didn't want to play.

He didn't want to eat cookies.

After all, he was crabby!

Crabby Carl Goes to School (cont.)

When Crabby Carl was a little older, he used to stand outside the front door and watch his sister playing with the next-door neighbors.

Angela said, "Carl, do you want to play?"

But Crabby Carl always said, "No!"

Crabby Carl Goes to School (cont.)

Crabby Carl's grandma looked out the window at him and said to his mother, "What is the matter with that child?"

His mother sighed, "I don't know. He is always crabby. It makes me sad."

"Tsk!" said Grandma. As Grandma left, Angela gave her a big hug and kiss.

Then Grandma turned to Carl and waited. But Carl did not hug or kiss his grandma goodbye. He just felt too crabby.

"Goodbye, Angela, dear," Grandma said, "Goodbye, Carl."

Carl said, "Hmph!"

Crabby Carl Goes to School (cont.)

Soon the day came for Carl to go to school.

His mother bought him a really great lunchbox with a big smiling face on the front.

Carl turned the lunchbox over and pretended the happy face was frowning, but he didn't let his mother see him do it.

132

Crabby Carl Goes to School (cont.)

Finally, the big day arrived—Carl's first day of school. His mother kissed him goodbye and told him she loved him. And off he went on the bus.

Crabby Carl Goes to School (cont.)

He sat next to a little red-haired girl carrying a teddy bear. "Hi," she said, "I'm Brittany Feddle. I'm five!"

Carl didn't say anything. He just turned his lunchbox over so it would frown.

But Brittany didn't notice the frowning lunchbox. She continued to smile. "Isn't it great to go someplace new and make new friends?"

Carl looked at the smiling girl who plainly was waiting for something in return. And Carl knew just what it was. Very slowly, after a long hard try, he turned the corners of his mouth up, just like the face on his lunchbox. It wasn't so hard to smile, after all.

Crabby Carl Goes to School (cont.)

"My name is Carl," he told Brittany. "I'm five, too."

Carl smiled a lot the first day of school, and by the end of the day he had made three friends.

Crabby Carl Goes to School (cont.)

When Carl went home that afternoon, he walked up the sidewalk, whistling and grinning. Carl's mother, watching from the window, nearly fell over.

Crabby Carl Goes to School (cont.)

"What's the matter, dear?" asked Carl's grandma.

"Some happy boy has stolen Carl's new lunchbox!" Angela cried.

"Wait! It's Carl!" said Carl's mother.

"Hi, everyone!" Carl put down his things and gave each of them a kiss.

"Hi, Grandma! Hi, Angela!" Then Carl gave each of them a hug, too.

"Where's Crabby Carl?" Angela asked.

"I don't know what you're talking about," said Carl, "but I learned a new game at school today. Want to eat some cookies and play?"

"Sure!" said Angela.

That day was just the beginning of Carl's good times.

 #2128 Getting Your Child Ready for School

"Tea Party" Game

Objective

In this activity, your child will gain social readiness for school by learning manners at a pretend tea party. This activity fosters politeness, knowledge about proper table manners, and awareness of other's feelings, as well as sensitivity and tactfulness.

What To Do

Young children love to play tea party, and there is much you can teach your child by creating a special "Tea Party" game for him. All you need for this is your already existing play-kitchen equipment. If your child doesn't have these kinds of toys, you can easily create a wonderful instructional tea party, using regular or disposable tableware.

Begin this activity by thinking about the kinds of manners you would like to reinforce with your child. Some preschoolers are still trying to learn to use a fork and spoon properly, and that is just fine. Concentrate on the kinds of social manners you would like your child to display when he or she is eating in school. Here is a list of some important basics for preschoolers:

- using a spoon and fork
- using a napkin
- asking for something politely
- asking to leave the table
- dealing with a food he or she doesn't like
- excusing oneself after burping
- making adults aware of food allergies

Set up a tea party for your child in which he or she can try some real food. Talk about polite manners and model what you mean. This can be a fun and interesting way to model correct behavior.

What To Say

I think it might be fun if we had a tea party and invited some of your teddy bears and dolls. I think we could buy a small cake or give them cookies and milk. What do you think? Let's set them up at the table here. Now, they will all need napkins, and we should tell them to try not to spill any food. I think that one bear might have burped. I can see we are going to have to teach him to say, "Excuse me!" (etc.)

Variations

Have your older children take part in the tea party game. Practice dining-out manners in fast food and other kid-friendly restaurants.

"Tea Party" Game (cont.)

Milestone Checklist

❑ My child understood what is meant by "good manners" on_____/_____/_____.

❑ My child explained manners orally on_____/_____/_____.

❑ My child demonstrated the proper use of a fork on_____/_____/_____.

❑ My child demonstrated the proper use of a spoon on_____/_____/_____.

❑ My child demonstrated the proper use of a napkin on_____/_____/_____.

❑ My child asked for something politely on_____/_____/_____.

❑ My child assisted in setting the table on_____/_____/_____.

❑ My child set the table alone on_____/_____/_____.

❑ My child communicated any food allergies orally on_____/_____/_____.

Our First Tea Party

What my child served:_____

My observations about my child's manners: _____

_____

Instructions I gave my child about manners:_____

_____

Results I have noticed: _____

_____

Our Second Tea Party

What my child served:_____

My observations about my child's manners: _____

_____

Instructions I gave my child about manners:_____

_____

Results I have noticed: _____

_____

Our Third Tea Party

What my child served:_____

My observations about my child's manners: _____

_____

Instructions I gave my child about manners:_____

_____

Results I have noticed: _____

_____

Good Manners Reward Chart

Objective

In this activity, your child gains social readiness for school by increasing the ability to be polite by learning to say "please" and "thank you." This activity fosters manners, empathy, kindness, and self-esteem.

What To Do

Make being polite a game that your child can win, as this will help motivate him or her and make the hard work of remembering manners more fun. Eventually, when your child goes to school, polite manners will help him or her get along far better with adults and other children.

Begin this activity, by talking with your child about the terms of good manners, e.g., "please" and "thank you." Then, make her a simple chart called "I Have Good Manners."

Each time your child remembers to say "please" or "thank you," or shows other excellent manners, add a star to the chart. When the chart is full, decide upon a small gift or privilege. This will make remembering manners a self–esteem–building exercise to enjoy.

What To Say

I really like it when you say "please" and "thank you." I feel good when you use good manners, and so do other people. So let's make it really fun. I will make a chart and every time you have really nice manners, we will add a gold star. After the whole chart is full of stars, we will go someplace special. Won't that be fun? Let's put the chart up in your room together.

Month					Year	
Sunday	Monday	Tuesday	Wednesday	Thursday	Friday	Saturday
		☆				
	☆				☆	
			☆			
	☆					☆

Variations

Use the manners chart to focus on different kinds of manners you would like to encourage. Or, use the chart for simple chores or other small responsibilities that your preschooler can fulfill. Remember to choose things your child can do so he or she can win and have a positive experience. Give stars for a good try as well as for a complete job.

Good Manners Reward Chart (cont.)

Milestone Checklist

☐ My child understood the words "please" and "thank you" and knows when they are said on_____/_____/_____.

☐ My child said "please" and "thank you" with prompting on_____/_____/_____.

☐ My child said "please" and "thank you" without prompting on_____/_____/_____.

☐ My child listened and responded to requests from me regarding manners on_____/_____/_____.

☐ I introduced the award chart to my child on_____/_____/_____.

☐ My child uses his or her reward chart consistently.

His or her response to this system was

_____

_____

_____

My desires regarding this motivational tool are

_____

_____

_____

Activity Repetitions

Change the reward chart monthly.

Month_____					Year_____	
Sunday	Monday	Tuesday	Wednesday	Thursday	Friday	Saturday

Using the Restroom

Objective

In this activity, your child will gain social readiness for school by learning how to use a public restroom with ease. This activity will foster your child's self-esteem and confidence as well as feelings of security and comfort.

What To Do

Can you imagine how upsetting it would be if you didn't know how to use a public restroom? As adults, we forget that this ordinary experience is new and troubling for preschoolers.

Begin this activity by making use of a public restroom a regular part of your travels with your child around town. But don't rush your child through the experience by doing everything for him or her. Let your child be increasingly responsible for the experience. For example, let him or her find the toilet seat cover and put it on, flush the toilet, and open and close the lock on the door. It may sound simplistic, but very often rushed parents don't think about letting their children do these tasks independently.

What To Say

You are getting so big, we should start to let you do everything when we go to the potty together. I am sure you are big enough to do a lot more. Then, when you get to school, you will be able to do it all by yourself. Won't that be great?

Variations

When your child gets ready to go to a new school and you take him or her to visit for the first time, be sure to ask about the restrooms. Let him or her have the experience of using the potty while you are there.

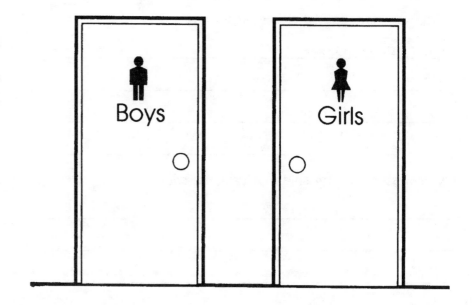

Using the Restroom (cont.)

Milestone Checklist	Date	What Happened	Positive Feedback
❑ My child determined when he or she needed to go to the restroom.	__/__/__	_____ _____	_____ _____
❑ My child understood the universal signs for "Men's" and "Women's" restrooms.		_____ _____	_____ _____
❑ My child could read the words "Boys" or "Men" and "Girls" or "Women" on ____/____/____.	__/__/__	_____ _____	_____ _____
❑ My child could latch the restroom door unassisted on____/____/____.		_____ _____	_____ _____
❑ My child could undress and dress unassisted on____/____/____.	__/__/__	_____ _____	_____ _____
❑ My child used a public restroom unassisted on____/____/____.		_____ _____	_____ _____

Activity Repetitions

Restroom Experience

Date and note the public restroom experiences your child has. Look for and praise improvements in mastery and competence whenever possible.

	Date	What Happened	Positive Feedback
	__/__/__	_____ _____ _____	_____ _____ _____
	__/__/__	_____ _____ _____	_____ _____ _____

Kitchen Timer Turns

Objective

In this activity, your child will gain social readiness for school by learning how to take turns by playing the kitchen timer game. This activity fosters empathy, understanding, caring, and concern for others, as well as a sense of fairness.

What To Do

Sharing is a learned skill. Children do not naturally know how to share nor should they share everything with everybody. However, in school there are many situations in which a child must share with courtesy and a good attitude. Sharing is really just another skill of politeness.

Begin this activity by purchasing a kitchen timer for your children to use. (If you have only one child, you or other family members can take turns with your child.)

In any situation when your child needs to take turns or share something, whether it is a toy or a game, keep the kitchen timer handy and ask your child and whomever else is involved to set the kitchen timer for a number of minutes and then take turns with the object when the timer goes off. Young children will think it is fun to set the timer, and the process becomes a game in and of itself.

What To Say

I have a timer for you to use so that it will be easier to take turns. Let's set it for ten minutes. When it goes off, you will hear a little bell. Now, would you like to try setting it? After the bell goes off, let your friend have the toy and set the timer again. This way it will be fair, and you will both get a turn.

Variations

Use the kitchen timer with your preschooler as a way of setting limits. For example, you might set it—or ask him or her to set it—one half an hour before bedtime or set it for the length of a rest or nap.

Kitchen Timer Turns (cont.)

Milestone Checklist

❑ My child showed an understanding of his or her own feelings and preferences.

❑ My child realized that others have different preferences than his or hers.

❑ My child showed concern for others' feelings.

❑ My child began to show a sense of empathy toward others.

❑ My child realized when he or she had hurt someone else.

❑ My child was able to apologize.

❑ My child was able to communicate his or her wishes appropriately.

❑ I introduced "Kitchen Timer Turns" to my child on_____/_____/_____.

(Observe your child taking turns using the timer on a number of occasions and note his or her progress here:

General Observations:

My child actively shared toys on_____/_____/_____.

My child was interested in taking turns on_____/_____/_____.

My child could set the timer alone on_____/_____/_____.

My child seems to play fair most of the time.

Activity Repetitions

#2_____/_____/_____

What I noticed about my child's ability and willingness to follow rules, take turns, and play fairly today:

_____

_____

_____

_____

#3_____/_____/_____

What I noticed about my child's ability and willingness to follow rules, take turns, and play fairly today:

_____

_____

_____

_____

What I Like About You

Objective

In this activity, your child will gain social readiness for school by beginning to notice what he or she likes about other people and becoming aware of others' good qualities by making a "What I Like About You" list. This activity fosters kindness, goodwill toward others, empathy, and tolerance.

What To Do

One of the positive signs of a young child's normal development is his or her ability to recognize that there are other people in the world! When children begin life, they are naturally self-centered, a stage which lasts until around age seven. However, it is important for them to consider the needs of others. The message will need to be repeated often until the child is able to fully understand.

In this activity, you and your child will create a "What I Like About You" list. Begin by talking with your child about different people and what is likable about each. Pick a specific person and, together with your child, think of as many likeable qualities as you can and write them down together. After writing each quality, talk about it and display the words you have written.

Do this activity repeatedly over a period of time. It may also be interesting for you to talk about yourselves and each other. Ask your child to make a list of his or her own likable qualities and then share your list. Soon your child will begin to take an active interest in other people. Here is an example:

What I Like About Grandma

She is nice.

She makes cookies.

She loves me.

She has pretty hair.

She is nice to animals.

What To Say

I was thinking about all of the wonderful things I like about Grandma. She is really a special person. Can you think of some things you like about her? I like her for making us cookies. What do you like about her?

Variations

Do this activity with your whole family as a dinner table exercise. It will be a positive experience for the whole family.

What I Like About You (cont.)

Milestone Checklist

☐ My child completed a "What I Like About You" list on _____/_____/_____for _____.

☐ My child completed a "What I Like About You" list on _____/_____/_____for me.

☐ My child completed a "What I Like About You" list on _____/_____/_____for himself or herself.

☐ My child demonstrated goodwill toward others.

☐ My child demonstrated kindness toward others.

☐ My child demonstrated empathy toward others.

☐ My child demonstrated tolerance toward others.

☐ My child chose_____for his or her first list and listed the following qualities:

_____

_____

_____

_____

Activity Repetitions

#2

My child made the following list about himself or herself:

_____ _____ _____

_____ _____ _____

_____ _____ _____

_____ _____ _____

_____ _____ _____

#3

My child made the following list about himself or herself:

_____ _____ _____

_____ _____ _____

_____ _____ _____

_____ _____ _____

(Compare the first and second lists for the same person, and talk about the differences with your child.)

Quiet Time

Objective

In this activity, your child will gain social readiness for school by becoming quiet and comfortable during a short, regular rest period by using a music or sound tape. This activity fosters physical and emotional self-control, self-confidence, and relaxation.

What To Do

Children need to be able to rest quietly for twenty to thirty minutes without being disruptive before entering kindergarten. For many children this comes naturally, but for others resting is a difficult, almost impossible task. By using a timed music tape, you can help your child learn to relax for a specific period of time.

Begin this activity by helping your child purchase a tape. There are a wide variety of tapes that can be purchased that feature relaxing music or sounds from natural environments such as the ocean or a forest. Ask your child which type will be most calming or record your own tape with your own home recorder.

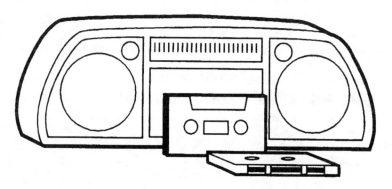

When selecting a tape, ask if you can listen to it before making a purchase. If not, read the label carefully to ensure that it is the type of tape you want. Look for a tape with a single side that runs about thirty minutes. Then play this tape for your child and take a rest time together. Talk quietly about the pretty music or sounds and how soothing they are. Talk with your child about how important it is to be able to rest when he or she goes to school and how the teacher will ask the children to rest so they have energy to get through the day. After the tape is over, tell your child that rest time is over and that it is time to do something active and fun.

What To Say

When you are old enough to go to school, you will have to rest every day. Rest time is when the children lie quietly on towels, pads, or cots. Sometimes the teacher might play music and sometimes she might read a story really quietly, but you have to stay there for the whole time and relax and not wiggle. So it might be fun if we practice resting. Let's get a tape of some really pretty music, and then we can try it.

Variations

Try the tape for a bedtime relaxation tape. Or take it to play on the road.

Quiet Time (cont.)

Milestone Checklist

☐ My child rested for five to ten minutes when asked on_____/_____/_____.

☐ My child rested for ten to twenty minutes when asked on_____/_____/_____.

☐ My child rested for twenty to forty minutes when asked on_____/_____/_____.

☐ My child has several methods to relax with which he or she is comfortable.

☐ My child feels energetic and calm after resting.

☐ My child chose the following taped sounds or music for rest time:_____

(Use the rest of the form to observe your child's rest attitudes on several occasions.)

Rest time_____/_____/_____

Music or sounds played:

_____

_____

Observations:

_____

_____

Rest time_____/_____/_____

Music or sounds played:

_____

_____

Observations:

_____

_____

Rest time_____/_____/_____

Music or sounds played:

_____

_____

Observations:

_____

_____

"Playing It Safe" Game

Objective

In this activity, your child will gain social readiness for school by learning about red, yellow, and green traffic lights and their significance. This activity fosters your child's sense of being safe on the street and in traffic. This activity also fosters an ability to follow directions and to understand cause and effect relationships, as well as a sense of mastery.

What To Do

When your child begins school, understanding the basic rules about traffic and pedestrian safety is very important. While this is an ongoing process for young children, it's never too early to begin reinforcing these rules.

Begin this activity by talking to your child about safety rules while you are out and about the town. When you stop in the car for a traffic light, for example, say, "Red means 'stop' and green means 'go'."

At home, construct simple "stop" and "go" signs and red, yellow, and green "traffic lights." You can make these simply with the following materials:

- cardboard
- tape and scissors
- red, green, and yellow construction paper
- craft sticks or several old rulers
- thick-point black felt pen

Stop And Go Game

Have your child stand at the end of the room. Then hold up a sign. Say, "Go!" Then, hold up the stop sign and say, "Stop!" Practice until your child knows the meaning of the words and has the coordination to stop and go upon command.

What To Say

Safety in the street is very important. We always have to remember to "stop, look, and listen" before crossing the street. Will you help me make some pretend traffic signs? Then we can play a "stop and go" game that will be really fun and help you learn safety rules.

Variations

Make additional traffic lights and play "Stop, Slow, and Go."

"Playing It Safe" Game (cont.)

Milestone Checklist

❑ My child recognized a "Stop" sign on_____/_____/_____.

❑ My child recognized a "Go" sign on_____/_____/_____.

❑ My child knew the significance of red lights
on_____/_____/_____.

❑ My child knew the significance of yellow lights
on_____/_____/_____.

❑ My child knew the significance of green lights
on_____/_____/_____.

❑ We played the "Stop and Go" game
on_____/_____/_____.

I observed this about my child's understanding of the game:

_____

I observed this about my child's ability to follow directions:

_____

I observed this about my child's motor skills during the game:

_____

Overall impressions about my child's ability to deal safely with traffic rules:

_____

Activity Repetitions

#2

I observed this about my child's understanding of the game:

_____

I observed this about my child's ability to follow directions:

_____

I observed this about my child's motor skills during the game:

_____

#3

I observed this about my child's understanding of the game:

_____

I observed this about my child's ability to follow directions:

_____

I observed this about my child's motor skills during the game:

_____

Paper Doll Family

Objective

In this activity, your child will gain social readiness by making paper dolls to represent important family members. This activity fosters awareness, interest, understanding of others, tolerance, and acceptance of individual differences.

What To Do

Children have been making paper dolls since paper was invented! But the paper dolls that you and your child will make for this activity are a little different because they will represent your actual family. As you and your child make these paper dolls, you will have an opportunity to talk with your child about impressions of family members and facts about their individual lives.

After the paper dolls are completed, you will be able to interact with or watch your child playing with these dolls. The words your child gives to the dolls may give you insight into his or her thoughts about others. You will be able to get a general sense of how he or she perceives his or her own treatment and place in the family.

Materials:

- construction paper
- scissors
- crayons
- glue
- other art supplies for decoration (optional)
- shoebox (for "doll house" and storage)

Directions: Just cut a simple paper doll shape and let your child decorate it.

What To Say

I have a fun idea! Let's make paper dolls of the whole family. We can make them out of paper and color them, and then we can play with them. Who would you like to make? We need us and we also need Daddy and Gramps. I will help you cut them out and then we will decorate them and add clothes.

Variations

Add favorite friends and animal dolls.

Paper Doll Family (cont.)

Milestone Checklist

☐ My child completed his or her doll family on_____/_____/_____.

☐ My child became aware of the other members of the family on_____/_____/_____.

☐ My child knew several things about what each member likes on_____/_____/_____.

☐ My child knew several things about what each member dislikes on_____/_____/_____.

☐ My child knew one thing each family member likes to do for fun on_____/_____/_____.

My child's dolls represent

_____

_____

What I noticed about the experience of making the dolls with my child:

_____

_____

Activity Repetitions

#2

I observed this about my child's doll-play experience:

_____

_____

_____

Why this is interesting:

_____

_____

_____

#3

I observed this about my child's doll-play experience:

_____

_____

_____

Why this is interesting:

_____

_____

_____

Playdates

Objective

In this activity, your child will gain social readiness for school by learning how to play with other children, share toys, and interact socially at home and in the homes of other children. This activity fosters self-esteem and the ability to act appropriately in a variety of situations.

What To Do

Just going outside to play with the neighborhood children seems to be a thing of the past, so many parents rely on a more structured plan of arranged playdates for their children. Set up a playdate schedule with one or more parents of preschoolers. Perhaps you can meet in each other's homes on a rotating basis every Wednesday morning from 10:00 A.M. until noon (or every Saturday morning in the case of parents who are employed outside of the home). You can serve coffee or tea to the adults and make it a social occasion for everyone. The children will benefit, too, by seeing their parents in a social situation.

- Meet ahead of time and set up some basic ground rules.

- You will each need and set up a child-safe and easily supervised play area, preferably indoors so you will not have to cancel in case of rain.

- There should be enough toys to go around and keep everyone busy. You can pool toys, if necessary. Bring along big toys like tricycles if you know the children will be playing outdoors and have a patio to ride around on.

- The host child should put away any toys that will not be shared during the playdate. These should include favorite possessions and anything breakable.

- Discuss the possibility of including a simple art activity each week. (Or maybe one parent would like to have an art activity when it is his or her turn to host.) Plan ahead to collect the necessary supplies.

- Decide if you will each serve a snack when it is your turn to host the playdate or if the children should bring their own. It might be fun to have children bring their own snacks since that is what they will do in school.

- The adults should stay for the whole playdate. The parent who is hosting the playdate should not be providing a free baby-sitting service. Besides, this is a perfect opportunity to observe your own child's social behavior.

What To Say

We are going to start having a playdate every week. Today we are going to your friend's house, and next week all the children will come to our house. You will be able to practice playing with other children the way you will play when you go to school.

Variations

Turn the playdates into holiday gatherings or parties when a child's birthday is near. If you let the children make hanging paper chains and decorate paper plates and napkins, they will have a wonderful time.

Playdates (cont.)

Milestone Checklist

☐ My child and I discussed and planned our playdate schedule on _____/_____/_____.

☐ My child is looking forward to our first playdate on _____/_____/_____.

☐ My child went to his or her first playdate in a child's home on _____/_____/_____.

☐ My child helped host our first playdate in our home on _____/_____/_____.

☐ My child participated in an art activity in another home on _____/_____/_____.

☐ My child helped set up an art activity in our home on _____/_____/_____.

We have decided to put away these toys when we host a playdate:

_____ _____ _____

_____ _____ _____

Activity Repetitions

Home of _____

My observations:

_____

_____

#2

Home of _____

My observations:

_____

_____

#3

Home of _____

My observations:

_____

_____

Meeting the Neighbors

Objective

In this activity, your child will gain emotional readiness by becoming familiar with your neighbors. This activity will foster your child's sense of security and safety in his or her own neighborhood, as well as give additional self-confidence in handling problems.

What To Do

It's amazing how many people don't know their neighbors these days. But when it comes to the comfort and safety of your child in your own neighborhood, it is necessary to meet them. The ideal goal is to have at least two neighbors on your street or in your building that your child can go to in case of an emergency.

Begin this activity by having your child say hello to the neighbors. When you do, remind your child of your neighbor's name. If you are new to the neighborhood and really don't know anyone, try these strategies to meet your neighbors quickly and easily:

- Take your child trick-or-treating and introduce yourself as you go.
- Go over with your phone number or business card and offer to be available to them in case of an emergency and suggest you trade phone numbers.
- Take part in any event that your neighbors do together. Block parties and light display contests are good ways to become familiar with neighbors.
- Take over holiday cookie plates.
- Share extra fruit from your fruit trees.
- Host an open house or neighborhood party.

What To Say

Hello, Janet, how are you? That is our neighbor, Janet. You should call her Mrs. Jones. She is always home in the afternoons because she is retired. Let's take her some of the extra tomatoes from our garden. She is a very nice lady. She told me she has a grandchild who is eleven years old. If we ever need help, we could go over to her house, and I am sure she would try to help us.

Variations

When the time comes, ask your neighbor directly if you may instruct your child to call on her in case of an emergency. A direct approach avoids confusion, and, if she doesn't want the responsibility, she can tell you.

156

Meeting the Neighbors (cont.)

Milestone Checklist

- ☐ My child knew the names of at least two neighbors on_____/_____/_____.
- ☐ My child recalled and said the names of two neighbors on_____/_____/_____.
- ☐ My child talked with at least two neighbors by_____/_____/_____.
- ☐ I spoke with my neighbors about emergencies on_____/_____/_____.
- ☐ I traded numbers with at least two neighbors on_____/_____/_____.
- ☐ I introduced my child to these neighbors:

_____phone (   ) _____

_____phone (   ) _____

_____phone (   ) _____

_____phone (   ) _____

- ☐ I discussed with my child when it is appropriate to go to the neighbors for help on _____/_____/_____.

My observations of this conversation are

_____

_____

_____

Activity Repetitions

#2

My child interacted with the neighbors in the following way:

_____

_____

_____

My impressions are

_____

_____

#3

My child interacted with the neighbors in the following way:

_____

_____

_____

My impressions are

_____

_____

_____

Helping Others

Objective

In this activity, your child will gain emotional readiness for school by learning the importance of helping others and having practical experience doing so. This activity will increase your child's sense of self-worth and confidence as well as his or her sense of empathy.

What To Do

Psychologists have discovered that while children do experience empathy at a young age, providing additional guidance can be helpful. In fact, the development of empathy is a sign of healthy psychological growth and is very important in helping your child become a person who can get along well with others.

Begin this activity by becoming aware of the opportunities to help others in your community. Talk with your child about how he or she would like to help others. Although preschoolers won't necessarily have logical or practical ideas about how they can help, it is still an important discussion topic.

Many children who watch public or educational television will be very concerned with topics like pollution and "saving the earth." And while there is, on some small level, something that a preschooler can do about pollution (for example, picking up litter or recycling cans), the important thing about this activity is to give your child something he or she can actually perform that will directly help someone.

Here are some simple suggestions:

- donating used toys or clothes
- donating canned goods to a food pantry
- helping a neighbor or an elderly relative perform other simple chores
- leaving a piggy bank in a prominent spot to collect money for charity
- helping his or her own family members

What To Say

I think it would be nice if we helped our neighbor take trash cans in and out because they are so heavy. I could ask permission, and we could do this chore every time the trash collection has finished. Would you like to help me?

Variations

Be aware as you choose a helping activity to be sure that it is not too stressful for your child. There are some situations that, while good experience for an older child, might cause a preschooler to worry, such as visiting someone who is extremely ill.

Helping Others (cont.)

Milestone Checklist

❑ My child understood the idea of helping others on_____/_____/_____.

❑ My child made suggestions or shared ideas about how to help others on_____/_____/_____.

❑ My child participated in helping others on_____/_____/_____.

❑ My child expressed positive attitudes about helping others on_____/_____/_____.

❑ My child and I discussed what we like to do together to help others.

❑ His or her suggestions today were

_____

❑ We have decided to do the following:

_____

on_____/_____/_____.

My child's feelings during this experience were

_____

_____

My child's comments after the experience were

_____

_____

Activity Repetitions

#2

Today (_____/_____/_____) we decided to do the following:

My child's feelings during this experience were

_____

_____

My child's comments after the experience were

_____

_____

#3

Today (_____/_____/_____) we decided to do the following:

My child's feelings during this experience were

_____

_____

My child's comments after the experience were

_____

_____

Bibliography

Bredekamp, Sue. (Ed.) **Developmentally Appropriate Practice in Early Childhood Programs Serving Children From Birth Through Age 8, Expanded Edition**. Washington, D.C.: National Association for the Education of Young Children, 1992.

Bredekamp, Sue & Teresa Rosegrant. (Eds.) **Reaching Potentials: Appropriate Curriculum and Assessment for Young Children, Volume 1.** Washington, D.C.: National Association for the Education of Young Children, 1992.

Charles, C. M. **Educational Psychology: The Instrumental Endeavor.** Saint Louis: The C. V. Mosby Company, 1976.

Goleman, Daniel. **Emotional Intelligence**. New York: Bantam Books, 1995.

Harrow, Anita J. **A Taxonomy of the Psychomotor Domain.** New York: David McKay Company, Inc, 1972.

Jones, Claudia. **Parents Are Teachers, Too: Enriching Your Child's First Six Years**. Charlotte, Vermont: Williamson Publishing Co. (Funk & Wagnall's Edition), 1996.

Kamii, Constance. (Ed.). **Achievement Testing in the Early Grades**. Washington, D.C.: National Association for the Education of Young Children, 1994.

Meisels, Samuel J. with Sally Atkins-Burnett. **Developmental Screening in Early Childhood: A Guide**. Washington, D.C.: National Association for the Education of Young Children, 1994.

Rich, Dorothy. **MegaSkills**. Boston: Houghton Mifflin Company, 1992.

Teacher Created Materials Resource

#465 **Childhood Assessment**